M000082292

West of Buffalo

Life in a Small Indiana Town

Sarah Hathaway Thomas

Sarah H. Thomas

november 2009

Copyright © 2009 Sarah Hathaway Thomas
All rights reserved.

ISBN: 1-4392-4802-8
ISBN-13: 9781439248027

To order additional copies, please contact us.
BookSurge
www.booksurge.com
1-866-308-6235
orders@booksurge.com

While attending my niece's wedding in Boston, I met an elderly woman. In the course of our conversation, I revealed that I was living in Indiana.

"My deah," she said, unapologetically, "my husband and I have been all over the world, but we've never been west of Buffalo."

Indiana is definitely "West of Buffalo".

(The incidents in this book really happened. The names of most of the people and places have been changed.)

PROLOGUE

When my son, Dan, was ten years old, he told me he didn't like it at home and thought he might run away.

"I'll miss you, Dan," I said, "but I'll be able to save a lot of money on food bills. What you really ought to do, though, is make sure I like it here, because what if I run away from home? What would you do then?"

Dan never mentioned leaving home after that. Ten-year-olds are easy to fool.

I never thought I would carry through on my threat, but in my early forties I did just that. I didn't run from my children: I left the town where I had been born and had lived nearly all of my life. I left my familiar surroundings, my friends and my aging mother, following my heart and not my head. Giving up a city of 100,000 for one that was not much more than a bend in the road was not the most rational decision I could have made, but it was an escape, which I needed at the time.

❧

It is said that certain animals bond with the first thing they see after birth. If it is a pleasant association, they return to this thing or place because it stimulates the production of endorphins, otherwise known as brain morphine. Scientists have termed this process "imprinting". Thus it must have been with my family. We just keep returning to Springfield, Illinois.

Springfield is the city of my birth. My mother's side of the family moved to Springfield shortly after Illinois entered the Union. My great-great grandfather made his fortune in Cuba, dealing in commodities his descendants neglected to discuss. Slaves and rum are two possibilities. In 1831, he settled in Springfield, because the land was fertile and cheap. He bought many acres of farmland and encouraged his relatives to follow him to central Illinois. He prospered and propagated and, eventually, in 1907, his great-grand-daughter, who was to become my mother, was born. The youngest by far of five children, she was the most adventuresome. She went East to college where she met Ben, who would become my dad. He was from Baltimore, Maryland, and had a Ph.D. in history. They moved to Birmingham, Alabama, where he taught at Birmingham Southern University.

By a fortuitous turn of fate, they ended up back in Springfield.

"I never thought I would return home again," my mother told me. "I introduced your dad to Logan Hay (a prominent Springfield citizen who was a lawyer and state senator) and he liked Ben. He was looking for a historian to work at the Abraham Lincoln Association, so back we came."

Like my mother, I went East to college. Springfield did not figure into my plans after school. Nonetheless, circumstances interfered and thwarted my efforts to leave.

On my 21st birthday, my father, who had been diagnosed with cancer, ended his life. Less than a year later, my only brother was diagnosed with schizophrenia and my only sister got married and moved to California. My mother was 49 years old when she was widowed and I could not imagine her all alone with the myriad of tragedies that had befallen her. I returned to Springfield, dutifully, sadly, but not begrudgingly.

I then topped off bad luck with stupidity and married the wrong man...also from Springfield. Fourteen years, three children, and one divorce later, I was still there, only poorer and with less latitude than before. I had a fun, low-paying job as the director of two preschools. My ex and I gave up our beautiful home and I moved into a tall, narrow house that leaned a little to one side. My endorphins told me I was reasonably happy in this town that was imprinted on my DNA.

Then religion, which provides comfort and solace to so many, began to give me problems. I never fully accepted Christianity, but I felt I should expose my children to it. I was tepid when it came to religion, but most of the people I knew seemed to get something out of it, so I tried it. I attended the same church as my mother, where I taught Sunday School and served as a deacon, all the time telling myself this was the right thing to do. With the exception of the divorce, I was following the instincts and imprinting laid out for me by my ancestors.

One day, Catherine Phelps, an acquaintance from my married days, asked if she could accompany me to church. She was beautiful, with blue eyes, blond hair, and a great figure. Her skin was creamy and flawless, like the skin I have requested God give me in my next life. Catherine taught Women's Studies at the local college and was a liberated woman. She did not mention bringing her husband and three children with her to church. I agreed to take her with me the following Sunday.

Luke Churchill, the minister at our proper Presbyterian Church, was a big, virile man with a fringe of red hair that encircled his bald head. He gave thoughtful, intellectual sermons and was active in the community.

On the Sunday I took Catherine to church with me, we sat near the front of the sanctuary on the pulpit side. A few minutes into the sermon Luke paused, momentarily losing his train of thought. I was surprised to see him looking straight at Catherine. I turned to look at her and she was gazing right back at him. She exhibited no embarrassment at causing a distraction. After a few seconds, Luke glanced down at his notes, searched for his place, and continued his homily. On the way home, Catherine told me she intended to ask Luke to speak about women in the Bible to her Women's Studies class.

I gave no more thought to this until several months later, when Catherine appeared at my door. She said she had to talk to me about a very important matter.

"Shortly after I went to church with you, I asked Luke to speak to my class," she said. "He came out the very next week. He was wonderful. The students loved him. Afterwards, we went for coffee and then...."

She paused. We were sitting at the picnic table in my back yard. I watched as she glanced behind her.

"Go on," I said. "No one is here."

She continued. "Then we went back to his house and went to bed."

I froze.

I wondered what she wanted from me. It was a full minute before I spoke.

"Why are you telling me this?" I asked.

"I think the church elders are having a meeting today. I am afraid they have heard about this and are going to discuss it at the meeting."

"And what do you think I can do about it?"

She didn't answer right away but never took her eyes off me. She eventually took a deep breath and said, "I don't know."

I had never before seen her unsure of herself. She was clearly frightened.

"Does your husband know about this?" I asked.

"Yes, he's involved, also. We have been partner-swapping."

I did not want to know about this. This was my minister and my church. I was anxious for her to leave. I needed to be alone to think about what I should do. "I'm sorry, Catherine," I said, while struggling to maintain my composure, "I can't think of a thing I can do." I stood up and made it clear she should go. For several nights, I barely slept. I had trouble concentrating at work. I wished Catherine had not confided in me. I couldn't ignore what she told me. I decided the only fair thing to do was to talk to Luke. I met him in his office at the church and asked him if the stories Catherine had told me were true.

"Yes, they are true," he said. "I believe in open marriage and free love and I am willing to debate their merits in an open forum." He continued by quoting the Bible to defend his position.

"St. Matthew said, 'That whosoever looketh upon a woman to lust after her hath committed adultery with her already in his heart. And if thy right eye offend thee, pluck it out, and cast it from thee.' Now, isn't that ridiculous?" he continued. "He must have been being facetious. No one would pluck out his own eye and throw it away. So he must have been kidding when he said that you shouldn't commit adultery."

"That's an interesting interpretation, Luke," I said.

"My wife, Abigail, agrees with me," he said. "In case you don't believe me, I'll call her right now and you can ask her." He reached for the phone on his desk.

"You don't get it, Luke," I said. "I don't care about Abigail. She isn't my minister. I am only concerned about what you do. Do you really think God approves of this?"

"Look, Sarah," he continued, "Presbyterians have rejected the vision of God as a vengeful God and have portrayed Him as loving and desirous of our happiness. "

"And He knows what makes you the happiest, doesn't He, Luke?" I said, barely masking my sarcasm.

He smiled and nodded. I stood up and left his office without saying goodbye. I now knew what Catherine had told me was true and I had to decide what to do with the information. It was a heavy burden.

Soon after my conversation with Luke, stories began circulating throughout the church about several members of the congregation who were involved in, or otherwise had knowledge of, the errant minister's escapades. A couple, whose three beautiful daughters' marriages had been presided over by Luke, reported he had propositioned their bridesmaids. There was also a story circulating about a nude party with him in attendance: The hostess had been regaled with laughter when she insisted on wearing an apron while cooking. Luke's weekly evening visits to a newly widowed church member looked suspicious. I was getting a whole new understanding of the term "lay members" of the church.

After much floor pacing, I went to the top two elders and told them what I knew. Their reaction? One of them didn't believe me and the other one said, "How do I know you aren't a woman scorned?"

In spite of the elders' indifference to the problem, the congregation, wise now to Luke's activities, began holding meetings to discuss Luke's future with our church. Luke was aware of this. He cornered me in the sanctuary one Sunday, while I was performing my duties as a deacon and preparing the altar for services.

"Sarah," he roared, as he loomed over me. "I think you should leave this church. There is another Presbyterian church in town and I think you would like it better than this one. You don't belong here."

I looked up at him. His long black robe and his face flushed with anger made him a frightening sight.

I swallowed hard. "Luke," I said with barely a quiver in my voice, "you are employed by me and the rest of this congregation. If you are unhappy with me, perhaps you are the one who ought to leave."

He had no reply and departed in a rage. Then I began to shake.

Luke's indiscretions could not be denied and he was eventually told by the congregation he had to leave. Soon after, he was defrocked. When questions arose about the glowing reports our church had received about him before he was hired, it was revealed that his previous church had given him a good recommendation because they wanted to get rid of him.

After Luke left and the situation cooled down at church, I sent my eldest daughter, Julie, merrily off to college, where she met a hamburger flipper she just had to have. When she left for her second year of school, she never enrolled and decided she was going to get married instead. No amount of talking would change her mind, so the two nineteen-year olds embarked on the rest of their lives together. My secure little world was on a downward spiral.

God had more surprises for me. He took away one of my beloved aunts. Having an unmarried aunt is like having an extra mother and I was fortunate enough to have two of them. They delighted in spoiling my brother, my sister and me when we were growing up. They lived with my grandmother, now deceased, and my crazy uncle in a big old house they called Westacre because it sat on an acre of land on the west edge of town. Now, one of them was gone and the other one had Alzheimer's and was in a nursing home. When the first aunt died, I discovered both of their estates had been grossly mismanaged by the bank, which was run by people who had known my family for generations. My sister and I had to hire a lawyer to get our inheritance, and the bankers, some of whom were my friends, were not happy with us.

While my aunt's estate was tied up with the lawyers, I decided I needed to make some changes in my life. I also needed money. I still had my son, Dan, and my daughter, Amy, at home to support and I started looking for a new job. The Sunday paper had an ad for someone to sell educational materials to schools. It was the only job I was remotely qualified for. I had never sold anything in my life except Girl Scout cookies, but I did have experience in the field of education, so I applied for the position and received a reply.

The job entailed working for two companies selling teaching aids to schools. Because the population in my area was sparse, I would have to carry several lines of materials in order to survive. Both companies wanted to interview me and they set up appointments to meet with me.

Then came the worst winter we had experienced in decades. Each week brought either a huge snowstorm or ice so thick the children skated in the streets. After several failed attempts and a harrowing 70-mile trip, I had my first interview. It went well, so I was then to be interviewed by Carsten O'Day, the district manager of the second company.

His deep, resonant voice curled my toes. He tried several times to make the 250-mile flight from northern Indiana to interview me, but the weather always interfered. After the third aborted attempt, he said, in reference to the terrain of the surrounding area, "I would drive down there, but the ocean's more interesting." Hmmmmmm…..a sexy voice and a sense of humor! What more could a girl want?

He never came.

Based on the opinion of the representative of the other company, Carsten decided I would work out fine. He hired me sight unseen and again made arrangements to meet with me to begin my training. Two days before he was to arrive, he got fired. That meant I got fired. And I hadn't even started yet. Even worse, I had resigned from my preschool job. I asked Carsten what was going to happen to him. Evidently, I was the only sales rep who was concerned about him, which made a big impression on him because all of the others were only concerned about themselves. I began working for the first company, but I needed to have another company to represent. Carsten tried to find a second line for me to carry and long telephone conversations ensued.

After a few months, we each began to get curious about the person on the other end of the phone line and he asked me for a picture. I foolishly agreed to send one, even though it occurred to me it could, quite possibly, end a relationship that had never gotten started. How could I have been so stupid? In a moment of inspiration, I went to my stack of *National Geographic*s and found a glorious picture of a young and beautiful African girl. It was a close-up of her head and torso, every inch of which was covered with tattoos, paint and jewelry. Her pendulous breasts hung to her waist. I placed the picture in a manila envelope and marked on the outside: "Photos-Do Not Bend". I enclosed a note that said, "This is the best picture I could find. Sorry about the sagging protuberances." It wasn't long before I received a reply.

"I got your wonderful picture, and don't worry about the sagging protuberances. Remember, it is better to have protuberated and sagged than never to have protuberated at all."

I had to meet this man.

෯෪

I finally met him in Chicago. He came over from Indiana and I from 200 miles south of the city. There he was. His big blue eyes were partially concealed by large horn-rimmed glasses. His hair was thick, gray and curly. His upper lip had a dent in it from his ever-present pipe and his smile exposed crooked teeth. He was neither tall nor short and had a round body with a slightly protruding tummy. His short, thick neck and sloping shoulders made him somewhat turtle-shaped.

He was a conservative dresser, typical of an Eastern college boy of the 50s. His tweed wool jacket was slightly rumpled. When he lit his pipe, I noticed he had strong, well-shaped hands and fingers, with the exception of one finger, which had been broken and never set.

I was not disappointed.

That night we dined under a large moose head at a nice Chicago restaurant and danced until the place closed. When he kissed me goodnight, I knew we would be seeing much more of each other.

I later visited him at his Indiana farm at the edge of a speck of a town named Preston. I can't remember what I thought when I first saw the scrubby land with the run-down farmhouse, but it didn't matter. It was spring and the budding green trees, rolling hills, and small pond were quiet and peaceful. I discovered things about him I liked: he was an only child who had excelled in school; he had received a full scholarship to a prestigious college in his native state of New York; he was a philosophy major. Our time together was blissful and afterwards Carsten sent me a poem by Sara Teasdale:

> Into my heart's treasury I placed a coin
> That time cannot take nor a thief purloin.
> Oh more than the minting of a well crowned king
> Is the safe-kept memory of a lovely thing.

I asked him to marry me.

ตจ

One and a half years later we married and I moved to the Indiana farm. I was running away from home, but I told myself I was running to Carsten. I refused to think about the enormous changes the move and the marriage would bring to my life. I only thought of it as my escape.

PARADISE FARM

My dad was a gentleman farmer. Originally a city boy from the East, he was remarkably successful at farming. My mother had inherited an ill-maintained farm.... the perfect venue for my dad to supplement his income while he wrote books about Abraham Lincoln and other personalities of the Civil War era.

He improved the farm and started herds of purebred cattle and hogs. He loved showing his cattle at fairs around the state and sleeping in the barns with the cows and the farmers.

"I'll bet I'm the only guy in those barns with a Ph.D.," he would say.

He also delighted in telling stories of his adventures on these trips. A great mimic, he would quote the farmers and the humorous things they said. It was a new world for him and he relished the richness of it.

On the farm he had two ponds dug and a shack built nearby where our family and my parents' friends and families would often spend weekends. The shack had no running water and no electricity, but that was part of the allure. Fishing and cards were the order of the day for the adults while the children caught grasshoppers for bait. They spit "tobacco" on our hands, which made us squeal and sometimes release them. We had an old flat bottomed metal boat we floated around on and there were woods to explore. I loved the farm and asked my parents if I could spend the summer with the tenant farmer and his family. They just laughed at me.

Carsten's farm was a small clump of land in northwest Indiana. It was on the outskirts of the tiny town of Preston. The remoteness alone was an attraction for me. I had had enough of lawyers, bankers and churches. The farm's allure would be overlooked by someone in her right mind. A long, rutted, dirt driveway led to the house, which was surrounded on three sides by corn and alfalfa fields. A shoddy little four-unit apartment building stood at the edge of the property. Called "Paradise Farm" by its owner, it would not have attracted many women. Its remoteness, the woods, the muddy, rutted driveway and the tumbledown house, were not what anyone would call appealing. Perhaps it was the owner, this strange and jovial fellow, who made it seem livable.

In some ways Carsten was like my dad. Both were from families of limited means who went through college on scholarships. Both were smart, funny and fun-loving. In appearance, they were of similar size and shape. They were city boys from the East who came into the possession of farms: my dad, because of his marriage, and Carsten, because of his divorce.

Carsten bought Paradise Farm for his two boys, Jeffrey and Martin. When he and his first wife, Cece, divorced, they were living in New Jersey. Cece, the youngest child of 13, hailed from the south Chicago area. She took the boys back to the Midwest to be close to her many siblings, and Carsten followed to be close to the boys.

The farm was Carsten's enticement for them. He thought they could fish, shoot skeet and bond as father and sons there. Both boys were unhappy with their father's remarriage and showed their disapproval by rarely coming to the farm or by promising to come and then canceling out at the last minute. In spite of this, Carsten adored them. They were both tall and blond. Jeffrey the Great had a facade of bravado…a macho "don't mess with me" presence. Martin the Magnificent seldom smiled and had a hint of darkness behind his blue eyes.

੨੦੶੬

The pond was another reason Carsten bought Paradise Farm. The previous owner of this fine property had dug a pond, which was a short walk from the house down a winding path. It was simply a hole in the ground with water in it. The excavated earth was piled around the edges. One small area had been leveled enough to allow an approach to the water. Legend had it that the day after the pond was dug, a group of locals asked if they could go fishing there. The owner readily agreed, and the visitors stayed all afternoon, bewildered when they didn't catch any fish.

Carsten was an avid fly fisherman as was his father before him. I have often thought the fishing gene must be inherited, for there seems to be no other reason to enjoy standing holding a pole and trying to outwit a fish. Carsten loved tying flies and could stand for hours casting. He tried to get me interested in it, but I do not have the fishing gene.

While on our honeymoon in Florida, he tried to teach me to cast.

"Just pretend there's a ball on the end of the pole and you're throwing it," he said. On my first cast, I hooked a large bridge and gave it up forever then and there.

Carsten took his ocean rod to Florida in a cardboard box that originally held school wall maps, because he did not have a case for it. He stood the box in a corner of our hotel room and one day it was gone. He was sure it had been stolen.

"Someone could have climbed up from the outside and come in through the balcony. We're only on the fifth floor," he said.

"Carsten," I said, "Who would want your fishing rod?"

"It's a really good rod," he explained.

We spent the next day visiting pawn shops. When we still could not find it, we asked the maid if she had seen it. The poor woman burst into tears.

"I threw it away," she sobbed. "I thought it was an empty box."

"Maybe it's still in the dumpster!" Carsten said.

He ran to the dumpster and I, the newlywed, stood by my man. He leaned in. Thinking he saw something, he leaned in farther. Finally, just his legs were sticking out of the dumpster. At that moment, a very attractive elderly couple walked by and, seeing his legs sticking out of the dumpster and me standing beside it, shook their heads and clucked their tongues at us. My embarrassment turned me into a blushing bride.

The rod was gone. The hotel bought him a new one and off we went in a rented car for more fishing. We bought minnows for bait and drove down Florida's west shore. The hot sun beat down on the car, which we returned after a few days. While flying home on the plane, Carsten began to chuckle.

"What are you laughing at?" I asked.

"The minnows!" He had trouble catching his breath. "Remember how hot the rental car was? We left the minnows in the back seat!"

Now Carsten had his own fishing hole and he prided himself on sharing his bounty. Essentially a large mud puddle, the pond was considered one of the major recreation spots in the area. He welcomed all of the locals who asked to fish in it.

Fishing in Indiana is not a seasonal activity. The locals fish all year round and ice fishing is considered a highlight. The town people told their friends about our pond and their friends told their friends. Soon a steady stream of cars, motorcycles and snowmobiles were driving past our house and heading for the pond. The more furtive interlopers went along the railroad track to the back corner of the farm, where they climbed the fence and proceeded to the pond without passing by the house. If I went down there in the winter to ice skate, I would find many ice fishermen hunched over the holes they had made in the ice. They became quite upset when I skated around their fishing holes. They asked me where I came from and were unembarrassed when I told them I lived there.

A 30-acre field bordered our house on three sides. The crops were rotated between corn and alfalfa. Directly across the driveway from the house, on the one side not planted in row crops, was an apple orchard. In the spring, the trees were flocked with beautiful white and pink blossoms that filled the air with a sweet aroma. This heavenly phenomenon lasted, on average, two days. The wind quickly dispersed the blossoms, and the trees, which were offshoots of offshoots, bore small, wormy apples, unfit for human consumption.

Springtime brought other delights. The woods were filled with white dogwood trees and a lone catalpa tree put forth lush blossoms. The ground was covered with May apples, trillium, lilies of the valley and bloodroot. There was a white trillium tucked away at the side of the path to the pond. It was hard to find, but a truly magnificent sight.

The tillable acres were rented to a dairy farmer who lived down the road. Because he had a large number of cows on his farm, he also had a large amount of manure. In an effort to improve the fertility of our sandy soil, he spread manure on it by what looked like a large barrel on its side with wheels. There was a wheel of some sort inside, which rotated when the contraption was pulled by a tractor. The manure flew in all directions out of the top of the barrel. Sometimes the farmer got distracted and forgot to plow the manure under. The smell and the flies permeated the house.

An unfinished building stood behind our house. A nice barn had stood there once, according to Carsten. A few years back, he took in a stray dog, who happened to be pregnant, and let her sleep in the barn. She eventually had her puppies and Carsten thoughtfully gave them a bed of straw and a space heater when the weather got cold. I don't know why he didn't know straw and space heaters don't mix, but common sense was never his forte. The ensuing fire marked the end of the barn, the mother dog and the puppies. The insurance company paid Carsten just enough to have a concrete foundation and floor poured and to have cinder blocks put about three feet high around the edges. It had been that way for several years when I arrived. He always referred to it as "the barn".

Every year Carsten made a few attempts at finishing the barn. He planned a two-story section in the center, with sections resembling lean-tos on each side. He actually got a start on the southernmost "wing" that was to be solar heated. Perhaps he realized solar heat would be safer than a space heater and straw. Carsten had studied up on solar energy and decided he would make large panels of a special Plexiglas material in the roof. These would admit the sun, that would heat water, which was to be stored in one gallon milk jugs. I was to save all of our empty milk jugs and store them in, or on, the barn. Because the partially finished part of the barn was filled with his tools and machine parts, I had to store the milk bottles in the other part of the barn, which didn't actually exist and was not protected from the elements. They all disintegrated before they were ever used as warming bottles.

I once heard a philosopher describe existentialism: "Picture a man in a rowboat in the middle of the ocean being pelted by wind, rain, lightning, snow and ice. He is there coping as best he can against all of these elements." I sometimes felt like that existential man, but on dry land. We were pelted with all of the elements God had to offer, but the biggest one was snow. We were far enough north to experience colder weather than what I was accustomed to and, also, we had huge snow falls. Located east of the southern tip of Lake Michigan, we got something called lake effect snow in addition to just plain old north country snow. Lake effect snow results from moisture in the lake rising and becoming snow, which is then dumped on land to the east. We were the recipients of much of this snow. One winter we had more snow than Alaska. Another winter we had a snow storm so big there was no mail in the entire area for a week. So much for the motto "Neither rain nor snow…….."

The United Parcel Service came five days a week to deliver and/or pick up packages for our business. Winter was a challenge for them. Their trucks are very light and had trouble gaining traction on our driveway when it was snow-covered. Our winding driveway was usually not plowed, although we tried to drive the tractor on it to pack the snow down. Sometimes the snow was too deep to do even that. When the snowplow on the road piled snow at the entrance to the driveway, we were blocked in. On those days, the UPS driver would come to the entrance of the driveway and we would get on the tractor with our outgoing packages. We would drive to the pile of snow and throw packages back and forth to the driver.

Because there were no buildings around us to stop the wind, we once got drifts so high Carsten, on his return home from a business trip, had to dig his way to the door. It was not unusual for us to be snowed in for days. When bad weather was predicted, the entire area gathered at the grocery stores in the nearest town of Bradford and stocked up. I was often one of the crowd.

One approaching storm caught up with me as I headed home with a car full of provisions. I was able to get to our driveway, but just barely. The drifts had already begun to form and I had to walk up the driveway, leaving the car near the road. I watched from the window as the snow completely covered my little blue station wagon. The next day people began to shovel out. We were still unable to leave the house, so I again observed the scene from the window. I watched helplessly as a large truck with a snowplow started up our driveway. I had no way of telling the driver he was about to plow up my car. He came closer and closer as I frantically tried to think of ways to alert the driver. Then, miraculously, he stopped.... inches away from my car. I later learned he happened to glimpse a small patch of shiny blue through the mound of snow and he was able to stop just in the nick of time.

Another winter brought a mysterious virus that was attacking people all over the state. It also brought huge snows. When we attended teachers' conventions, we heard tales of sick people being airlifted out of snowbound houses and taken to the hospital.

Then Carsten got the virus. He lay in bed, limp and feverish. The snow came floating down...one foot deep, then a foot and a half. The wind picked up and the farm looked like one of those glass balls with the snow swirling inside. I felt totally helpless.

A call to the doctor was of no help, because the doctor said he could prescribe medicine, but he had no way of getting it to us. Still the snow fell and the wind blew.

The minister of the local church called to see how we were. I told him about our predicament and he said he had recently recovered from the awful virus and still had some medicine left.

"Thanks," I said, "But there is no way to get it here."

"I know a kid with a snowmobile. I'll send him over," he said.

True to his word, he did send the medicine and I watched in anticipation as the boy on the snowmobile approached. Then he stopped about half way up the driveway. He was stuck! He could go no farther. The heroic effort had failed. Carsten still lay sweating and aching in bed.

After a few days, Carsten began to rally and was able to get out of bed but was still weak and exhausted. I was stir crazy. I had to get out of the house. I also needed groceries. I bundled up in a parka with a hood, put on high boots, got a backpack and headed for the little grocery store in Preston. It took me about half an hour to make the half-mile trip. I bought milk, bread, a few cans of soup and orange juice, which was about all the store had to offer. I put them in the backpack and started home.

The wind started to blow again before I could get there. Drifts began to form and suddenly I found myself in snow over my knees. I stood on one foot and tried to lift my other foot over the snow. I could not do it. I found it is impossible to walk in snow above my knees. I tried pushing my legs forward through the snow, but made little or no progress. I headed toward areas that looked not quite as deep, but they were only dips in the terrain. The snow was over my knees wherever I went. I began to panic. It did not help matters to have a heavy load on my back on the return trip. I pushed my way through the snow for at least forty-five minutes and did not get any closer to home. Then I saw Carsten, outside on the porch in his bathrobe with a parka over his shoulders, telling me I could make it. I pushed and shoved my way through the snow. When I got close enough, Carsten held a long stick out for me to hold on to and I was able to pull myself on to the porch. I would never again try to walk in snow over my knees.

Carsten was a faithful reader of *Organic Gardening* magazine. He felt this qualified him as a farmer, or at least a master gardener. He spent hours planting seeds and surrounding them with marigolds to keep the bugs away, dried blood to keep the deer away, and milky spoor to kill grubs. Lady bugs killed aphids and praying mantises controlled flies, beetles, moths and cutworms. After plying the garden with all of those prophylactic organisms, he seemed to lose interest and neglected to weed it. The weeds thrived and soon it was impossible to tell what had been planted. I called it the "secret garden".

He planted asparagus crowns, even though asparagus grew wild all around us. He had read in *Organic Gardening* that asparagus originated in the ocean, so he poured salt water on the plants. That might be the reason asparagus did better unattended in the wild than it ever did in his garden.

He also had some strawberry plants in raised beds. They never yielded many berries, which was a great disappointment, as we both loved strawberries. "God could have made a better berry, but he didn't," Carsten said.

Carsten had a few successes, though. He was good at raising tomatoes and squash. The problem with tomatoes was, at exactly 4 p.m. every day, the mosquitoes emerged from wherever mosquitoes hide during the day and guarded those tomatoes with stingers the size of darts. It was just about the same time I needed tomatoes for dinner. A mad dash, while covered with insect repellent and a large hat, was required to retrieve a tomato.

To grow squash, the seeds should be placed in small mounds far enough apart to get a tractor and disc through to cultivate them. Carsten enjoyed riding his ancient Harvester Farmall M tractor around the squash plants, dragging an old disc that looked like it had been run over by a herd of buffalo. Thus, the squash section of the garden was kept weeded.

One year Carsten decided he was tired of growing acorn and butternut squash, and he planted Blue Hubbard squash. I had never heard of them and paid little attention when he planted them. They did exceptionally well and grew......and grew.....and grew. They got as big as pumpkins; there we were with about thirty of those things. Carsten was delighted. This had been one of his greatest gardening feats.

"Let's have one for dinner tonight," he suggested one fall afternoon.

I thought we might as well, since we had so many of them, but I had no idea where to begin.

"First of all, how do you cut one up?" I asked Carsten.

He had a ready answer. "You just throw it on the sidewalk."

I picked one up, remembering to bend my knees and lift with my whole body. The risk of back and arm injury was high. I then heaved it onto the sidewalk, and it did, indeed, break into about five pieces. These were still too large to put on the stove, so I cut them up into smaller pieces and put them into a pan to boil. Actually, I put them into about four pans; there was enough squash to feed at least half of the town. We ate a lot of squash that night. Unfortunately, it was not a gourmet's delight. The squash was tasteless and required much salt and butter to make it palatable.

All fall those squash lay in the garden. I was not going to go through the squash-tossing process again for a dish which was nearly inedible. In spite of Carsten's insistence that they really weren't so bad and we shouldn't let good food go to waste, I held my ground and refused to cook them.

Carsten's animal instincts took over when winter neared. He felt the need to stockpile food in case we were attacked by the Russians and couldn't get to the store. I assured him our Indiana town of 200 people was probably not a high priority on the Russians' list, but he was adamant. The fact that our town wasn't on most maps did not make him waiver. He gathered up the remaining squash and put them in his oversized wheelbarrow.

"Where are you going with those?" I asked.

"Down cellar," he replied. (His Eastern upbringing was betrayed by the two expressions, "down cellar" and "going to hospital".)

He pushed the wheelbarrow to the back of the house and proceeded to lower the huge load down the outside stairway to the basement.

"I need help here!" he shouted impatiently, as if the whole thing were my idea.

I ran to his aid and he told me to get in front of the wheelbarrow to keep it from going down the stairs too fast. I did as I was told, but the load was so heavy it took all of my strength to keep it from rolling over me.

"I can just see the headlines in the paper tomorrow," I yelled. "Local Woman Squashed By Squash!"

We got the squash down into the basement without a major mishap and there they stayed until I noticed we were getting a large number of fruit flies in the house. They emanated from the squash, and in the end, we threw them all out just as they were beginning to turn to mush. Thus ended one of Carsten's most successful gardening ventures.

Carsten really did love gardening...at least he loved working in the soil and planting things. The tending afterwards was the part that was often neglected. I had never planted anything but flowers. Watching him work the soil lovingly and read seed catalogues with great pleasure made me decide to help him and see if I liked it. He was happy to have a helper and together we turned over the soil in the garden. After crumbling it up into a fine consistency, we planted beans in a beautiful, straight row. We then planted marigolds along each side of the row and Carsten sprinkled it with dried blood. It was all organic and beautiful. Surprisingly, I enjoyed the experience and felt a real sense of accomplishment at the end of the day.

I always admire my own work. If I paint or wallpaper a room in the house, I get up in the middle of the night to look at it. If I tile a bathroom, I go in and feel the cold, smooth tiles for days after I finish the job. So of course, on the day after we planted the beans, I returned home from work and headed straight for the garden. I did not expect to see the beans sprouting. I just wanted to admire the freshly tilled soil and the neat rows of marigolds. Instead, I found a row of deep round holes where the seeds had been planted. It looked as if someone had taken a post hole digger and dug up the entire garden. I looked around to see if the perpetrator of this terrible deed was nearby. I spotted her, standing a few yards away, staring at me and calmly chewing her cud: the neighbor's cow had gotten through the fence and walked in a straight and deliberate line through all of our hard work from the day before.

"What does *Organic Gardening* recommend for preventing cattle infestation?" I asked Carsten when he returned home.

When we went back to Carsten's home town and told people we lived on a 57-acre farm, they were impressed. To Easterners, 57 acres seems huge. To someone in the Midwest, it sounds like a large back yard.

Carsten realized it wasn't a big farm, but he somehow felt it should be generating large amounts of money and he was constantly looking for different ways to make it pay. Corn and alfalfa were not the kind of cash crop he wanted. He thought walnut trees might work, because they had such valuable wood and were becoming scarce. The only problem was they took about fifty years to be big enough to harvest. In spite of this, he planted quite a few walnut trees, with the idea his grandchildren, of which he had none, would someday become wealthy from them. He also gave some thought to growing Christmas trees, but when he learned how much care they required, he abandoned the idea. He briefly considered ginseng, because it needed to be planted in watery areas and he had the ideal location: the pond. Ginseng was considered by some to be an aphrodisiac, so he was sure there would be a huge demand for it. He abandoned that idea for reasons unknown. He was even tempted to allow a paintball club to use the farm one weekend a month for their paintball war games. They would pay a nice price to use the property, but when he thought about the disruption it would cause, he decided against it.

In the 1980s, farmers were facing hard times. Fuel prices were high. Crop prices were low. Overproduction, declining land values and high interest rates added to the farmers' woes. Seeing an opportunity and a need, two men from Minnesota, motivated by Christian charity enhanced with capitalist greed, set out to save the farmers by introducing a new crop: Jerusalem artichokes. They are neither artichokes nor from Jerusalem. They are from the sunflower family and have an edible tuber. The tuber is white and about the size of an Idaho potato. It has high fructose content, a desirable asset for making ethanol. These two men were sure they had found the answer to the energy crisis and the farm crisis, so they set out to save the country with their new discovery. They formed a company called American Energy Farming Systems (AEFS) and flooded the Midwest with salesmen.

Carsten came home one day highly agitated. He had picked up a flyer at the farm store. It read:

7 COMPLETE REASONS TO GROW JERUSALEM ARTI-CHOKES. JOIN OTHERS WHO ARE BECOMING ENERGY CONSCIOUS BY PLANTING JERUSALEM ARTICHOKES
1. America's number 1 alcohol fuel and fructose sugar crop!
.....each ton...yields 22 gallons of 200 proof alcohol (etha-nol)...
2. High protein livestock crop!
....Cattle, dairy cows, horses, sheep, poultry and pigs all like the Jerusalem artichoke.
3. Easy to grow!
....One thousand pounds of seed stock tubers yields between 10,000 and 14,000 plants
per acre....
4. A "double portion" crop!
Plant growth above ground is matched by underground growth....
5. Tubers are winter hardy!
...can be harvested in the fall or left in the ground for winter storage and spring harvest....use
as Fuel, Food or Feed.
6. "Goodbye" to expensive fertilizer, herbicides and insecti-cides!
....Ninety percent of its growth comes from air, sunshine and water...not affected by insects
and is resistant to disease. No herbicides are necessary....
7. The number for completion!
Growers only need to purchase the tuber seed stock one time. From the initial crop, farmers will have an abundance of seed tubers for acreage expansion. Since some tubers al-ways remain in the ground at harvest time, next year's seed

crop is already planted. WHAT A PERFECT WAY TO COM-
PLETE A CROP SEASON!

He decided to investigate further. The promises only got
more appealing to him…and less appealing to me. The startup
costs were high: $1,000 per acre.

"But you only buy enough for ten acres," Carsten argued.
"Those ten acres produce 45-65 tons of tubers! You don't have to
replant, because they are a perennial. They are drought and frost
resistant and need very little fertilizer. You can then sell the seeds
to other farmers who do the same thing. It could solve the energy
crisis."

"Are these people from Egypt?" I asked.

"What do you mean?" Carsten was sounding exasperated.

"It sounds like they're selling pyramid schemes."

"Don't be such a pessimist," Carsten scolded. "All your people
ever think about is raising corn and beans. And where has that gotten you? This is revolutionary."

I wish I could say I told him there were not yet any ethanol
plants to process the fructose. I wish I could say I wisely reminded
him it had taken thirty years for soy beans to become a cash crop….
that there had to be machines developed for planting, cultivating
and harvesting, markets developed to sell to, products developed
to use the crop. I didn't. I only humored him and let him extol the
virtues of this plant previously thought to be a weed.

"Ralph Waldo Emerson said, 'A weed is a plant whose virtues
are not yet discovered," Carsten told me.

Carsten, who was a salesman himself, often nudged the truth
a little when he was selling. He was a talented salesman and I once
told him he could probably sell bikinis to the Eskimos. He was also
the biggest pushover I had ever known; oblivious to the fact other
salesmen will also stretch the truth to sell their products to him.
He was sure he had finally found a crop that would make him rich.
He planted a few Jerusalem artichokes in his vegetable garden,

just to see what they were like. They were also touted as a delicious vegetable, so we ate a few. Not only were they tough, but they had a slightly acrid taste. We soon discovered they produced another kind of gas.

"Since these are being advertised as a food source for livestock, do you suppose they will have the same flatulent effect on pigs and cows?" I asked. "Maybe their gas can be captured and used for fuel, just like ethanol."

"Ha, ha," Carsten replied sarcastically.

I didn't think they would become very popular as a source of nutrition for humans. Carsten was convinced he could still make a fortune off of them.

His enthusiasm for this crop did not diminish as fast it had for the others, and he went ahead with plans to buy the plants. A salesman was going to be in the area soon and he could begin planting right away. On the magic day he was scheduled to pay for and pick up the artichokes, he received a phone call from a friend of his.

"There's an article about Jerusalem artichokes in the Indianapolis newspaper," the friend said. "It tells about this huge scam that is going on. There is no demand for them, the marketing scheme is a pyramid, and the owners of the company have been arrested for fraud."

Carsten was crushed. He thought he had found the answer to creating great wealth and it disappeared with one brief phone call.

Further government investigation uncovered the fraudulent claims of the company. Because of their irregular size and shape, the artichokes are not easily harvested, stored or processed. They are most successfully harvested by hand-digging. They spread and are not easily eradicated. Also, no Jerusalem artichoke processing plants were in existence, and no ethanol had ever been produced from them.

We later read about the founders of the company being tried and jailed. They were found guilty of selling a product having no real use other than to propagate more of the product.

Instead of being a great source of income, Paradise Farm was a magnet. The pond was the biggest attraction, but other aspects of the place drew people to it. Hunters stalked in the woods. Teens planted marijuana along a remote fence row. I found glue-sniffing paraphernalia under some bushes. A man, whom we had never seen before, drove his tractor over to our farm, uprooted a sassafras tree, took the fragrant root, and left the fallen tree on the roadside. A florist from the neighboring town of Bradford brought a ladder and harvested the bittersweet which grew abundantly at the end of our driveway.

Carsten was generous about sharing and was not nearly as perturbed as I with the intruders. I begged him to stop letting people on the property, explaining I was often home alone. Coping with the interlopers was hard enough when he was there, but when I was alone, I was sometimes frightened.

"Can't you post 'No Trespassing' signs?" I asked.

"I tried that once, but people just tore them down. Then I figured I should just let them fish. This land is only rented, you know. "

"Rented? What are you talking about?"

"Oh, I own it now, but I'm only going to be on this earth a little while and I shouldn't be covetous about the land. Land is something you inhabit for a brief moment in time. It's here for us all to enjoy. It is something that we, as stewards, must take care of. We can't think of it as something we really own and can do with what we wish."

It was sometimes difficult to be married to a philosopher.

MY MASTER

The house I now shared with Carsten was built circa 1840. He called it "The Hovel". Carsten's description of it as "architecturally insignificant" was an understatement. It should have been listed on the National Register of Historic Places because not many so crudely built houses from that time period are still standing.

"What was it about this place made you buy it?" I asked Carsten.

"I never really looked at the house," he explained. "I just loved the land."

The old house was asphalt-shingled, sad looking and barely habitable. A weeping willow tree, its roots slowly pushing up the sidewalk and concrete platform at the entry to the kitchen, harbored a family of Baltimore orioles in its drooping branches. Unfortunately, the tree died shortly after my arrival and the orioles were never seen again. The sidewalk, however, remained askew for years come.

Four round pillars with peeling paint graced the front porch. They were hollow and sparrows had pecked holes in them in order to build their nests inside. The front door off of the porch was never used.

The interior of the house was no better. The side door opened into an inefficient kitchen with red painted cabinets. A wood burning stove for heat, not cooking, stood in the corner. Most of the heat rose to the open rafters in the ceiling. Birds occasionally came down the stovepipe to the wood stove. They did not fall into the fire because Carsten had installed a blower on the stovepipe. The birds got no farther than the blower and there they fluttered, unable to go up or down. Carsten had to go up on the roof and remove the cap on the stovepipe to release the hapless birds.

The rest of the house consisted of a living room with a small room off of it (I never could figure out if it was a room or a closet), a small bedroom adjacent to the kitchen and a laundry room to the rear of the kitchen. Huge hunks of plaster had fallen off the laundry room wall, exposing the wood lathe. The bedroom off the kitchen had been a lean-to in its former life, but had been refurbished with cheap paneling on the walls and a half bath had been added. A full bathroom was off of the living room. It had a blue bathtub, toilet and sink and a slightly rusted metal shower with a cement floor. The door to the bathroom often jammed and, more than once, I had to exit by climbing out of the window.

A door in the bathroom led to a basement. Carsten called it a Michigan basement. It was basically a hole underneath the house with a dirt floor and large rocks for walls. Its purpose was never revealed to me.

Carsten's ex-wife kept all of their furniture when they divorced, so The Hovel was furnished with discarded items from Carsten's friends and relatives and supplemented by purchases from the Salvation Army. The living room carpet was brown tweed with a large stain in the middle. Built-in bookcases, overflowing with books, filled one wall. A large picture window looked out toward the field and apartments. One of Carsten's most prized possessions, his chain saw, was neatly placed in the corner.

The upstairs consisted of one large room with a worn linoleum floor which was our bedroom. A mattress on a metal bed frame and a Salvation Army dresser were the only furnishings. A bare light bulb in the middle of the ceiling supplemented the light from the two windows. Carsten told me once, when his boys were visiting, they were so tired at the end of the day no one would get up and turn out the light. They ended up shooting it out with a BB gun. In the middle of the night they were too lazy to go downstairs to answer nature's call, so they peed out the window. Something about this place made that seem reasonable.

The mechanicals of the house were, at best, inadequate. The water was supplied by a well in the side yard pumped by an ancient pump, which periodically stopped and had to be restarted by sliding the heavy concrete cover to one side and hitting the mechanism with a broom handle. Even when it was in good working condition, the pump was so weak we had hardly any water pressure. The washing machine took an hour to fill and the well water was rusty, so our clothes were covered with tiny brown dots. The septic tank overflowed so often Carsten bought his own septic pump. Finally we had the tank replaced and found it had been installed upside down. The intake was below the outflow, making it basically a holding tank.

The ancient furnace burned stinky oil, which was stored in a large black tank in the yard outside the kitchen window. It barely heated the first floor and had to be supplemented by the wood stove. Carsten sometimes forgot to have the oil tank filled and then we had to rely solely on the wood stove for warmth. The bedroom upstairs was never heated. If I put a glass of water by my bed, it was often frozen in the morning.

We shared the house with many "critters". Mice could be heard scampering in the walls. I had brought our cat, Clawdia, with me and she proved to be invaluable in controlling the mouse population. She had been a city cat, but now turned into a wonderful "mouser". She was proud of her accomplishments and shared her catches with us. Once when I went out of town, she carefully placed a dead mouse on my pillow so Carsten would have company. Another time, when I was away, she put two mice on the breakfast table: one at my place and one at Carsten's. Nine dead mice, victims of a raid by Clawdia, lay outside the kitchen door one morning. We called it "The Preston Massacre".

Woodchucks settled in under the house. Unlike me, the woodchucks seemed to have found a use for the Michigan Basement. They exited early in the morning and Carsten would sometimes intercept them as they were returning. I still have visions of him in a plaid nightshirt I had given him, running outside on his skinny, hairy legs, arms flailing, trying to scare them away. They would dodge and weave and outmaneuver him every time, squeezing into the hole leading to their home.

We didn't want to kill the animals because they might die under the house and create a malodorous situation. Therefore, Carsten spent many hours devising schemes to make them leave. One plan was to play very loudly the worst hard rock music he could find on the radio. The woodchucks were unaffected by this, but it nearly made me leave. Carsten saw his opportunity to decrease the woodchuck population one day when the entire family of five—daddy, mommy and babies—sat on a log near the apple orchard in stair-step order, staring at him. He got his shotgun, aimed, and then did not have the heart to finish the job. We were not successful in plugging up their hole for several years.

Grackles—pesty, squawking, black, iridescent birds—found a hole in the upstairs and nested in a niche we could barely reach. They made themselves at home and even hatched a brood of fledglings. When we found them, we lit smoke bombs and firecrackers in their hole, but they were not deterred. They were totally unafraid of us. Carsten's reputation as a softy must have reached them. They finally left of their own accord, probably to move to more upscale housing. We were then able to plug up their hole.

Once, while installing insulation above the kitchen, I found a paper-wasp nest as big as a beach ball. It was so big I could not remove it and simply put the insulation around it. Luckily, it had been abandoned years earlier.

Wasps were everywhere around the house and barn. Some lived behind the shutters of the house. Mud daubers made their mud houses on the walls of the barn.

Hundreds of red and black box elder beetles basked in the sun on the side of the house, refreshed by the periodic mist of bug spray I doused them with. Their purpose in life, good or bad, was a mystery and nothing would repel them.

One day a large snake caught a toad and decided to swallow it right in front of our side door. Carsten came home and saw the snake, jaws unhinged, with the toad's head and front legs waving frantically out of its mouth. I was inside, oblivious to the gruesome event occurring outside. Carsten was able to get his shotgun and, because he hated and feared snakes, he was able to shoot this time. The snake died and the toad jumped out....snatched from the jaws of hell.

The residents of Preston who had lived there all of their lives told us some of the history of our house. "One family that lived there used to have a huge party for the whole town every year."

I was amazed because, although the town was not large, this house was quite small and surely could not accommodate the entire community.

"They just took all of the furniture out," the locals explained, "and we danced and sang in there all night. It was the best event of the year."

We learned more of its history when a nice-looking, middle-aged couple came to our door one summer afternoon. They told us they were from the state of Washington. The lady apologized for popping in unexpectedly. She told us she was doing her genealogy and found some of her earliest American ancestors had lived in this house.

Carsten happened to be mad at me that day. He decided to annoy me by wearing an outfit my daughter, Amy, and I had gotten him for a joke at the local Goodwill store. It consisted of vomit green plaid polyester pants with a matching green shirt, a wide white belt, an orange striped tie and white patent leather shoes. For some reason, he thought the wearing of this outfit would emphasize how angry he was with me. When he ushered this very normal looking couple into the house, I looked at him and the crude house our visitor seemed nostalgic about. I started to explain how we were in the process of fixing up the house and it must have looked better 150 years ago. I also wanted to explain that my husband didn't always look like the poster boy for "What Not to Wear". I then thought better of it. Why bother? I enjoyed watching him try to act like the master of the house in his stupid outfit.

The house that seemed adequate for Carsten was certainly not one I could live in. He realized this, and shortly after our wedding, we made plans to add on to it. We had very little money and hired a contractor to build a shell of an addition out from the kitchen. It was to consist of a basement, an expansion of the kitchen, a new living room, a dining room, and a downstairs bedroom with a bath. Two bedrooms and another bath were to go upstairs above the living room and dining room. There would be a new furnace and hot water heater. The old living room would become our office. We were to add the drywall, the flooring, the plumbing and electricity, the trim and detail work and the pipes for the hot water heat. We were also to put siding on the outside and paint the exterior and interior.

The contractor dug the basement and then arranged to have the concrete poured. The concrete workers arrived on the appointed day and listened to the weather forecast.

"It's gonna rain," they said.

"Are you sure?" I asked. It was cloudy, but the clouds were not dark.

"The weatherman said so," they told me. They then left, promising they would return the next day. It did not rain all day.

They came back the following day, as promised, and poured the floor. By 3 p.m. they had finished and they packed up and left. At 3:10 p.m., the sky released the rain it had been saving up from the day before. Rain fell in sheets all afternoon and into the evening. In the morning we sadly viewed our basement floor, which was now badly dimpled. The workmen returned and scratched their heads. They were at a loss to know what to do. I asked them if it would be possible to pour a thin layer of new cement over the old. They said they thought they could, so we got our basement floor, although the basement was not as deep as had originally been planned.

At least the contractor could now start building upward. I began to have hopes for the place as I watched the studs and sub-floors and windows go into place.

The day finally came when the addition was enclosed and we could tear out the wall between the kitchen and the new section of the house. Armed with crowbars and mallets, we attacked the wall. The old plaster and lathe crumbled around our feet as we smashed it. When we saw the result, we gasped. The new floor was about four inches higher than the old one. Because we were enlarging the kitchen into part of the new addition, we now had a step up in the middle of the kitchen floor. The contractor explained he had forgotten to figure in the height of the sill around the top of the basement walls.

We had to learn to live with it. Nothing could be done short of tearing down everything and starting over. That might not have helped either because the old house was uneven and the rise in the kitchen was higher on one side than the other.

Carsten and I set out to finish the addition. He was very handy, but his skills had never been put to a test this demanding. He wired and plumbed it. Together we insulated it. He ran the pipes for hot water heat. I became inured to his outbursts and expletives. I had never before known Jesus Christ had a middle name that started with "F".

The day we hung drywall in one of the upstairs bedrooms was the day I almost gave up on the project. It took both of us together using every bit of strength we had to lift the heavy four-by-eight foot panels into place and screw them to the studs. Carsten constructed a T-shaped contraption made of wood for holding the ceiling panels in place until they could be screwed in. Then tape and "mud" had to be applied to the seams. Three coats of mud were applied with a day or two of drying time in between. After the final application, the seams had to be sanded until perfectly smooth, which produced a fine white powder that floated into every nook and cranny in the house. When we finished the room, I said we would either hire out the rest of the dry walling job, or we would do without walls. I would never go through that again. Carsten agreed.

After we had walls installed by a professional drywaller, the projects became a little more interesting. We installed trim and painted and wallpapered the walls. We located a kitchen cabinet company with a demo kitchen for sale and Carsten installed it. We sided the house with redwood and painted the trim a cream color, which was very appealing. A man who lived on a farm a few miles away sold interior door "seconds" out of his barn. For ten dollars a piece, we purchased hollow core interior doors which looked like paneled doors. As we loaded the doors into our station wagon, two other customers, a middle-aged couple, stood and watched. After silently observing us for some time, the man turned to his wife and said, "Don't know why they want them fancy doors. Them flat doors work just as good."

Carsten and I did try, with what little resources we had, to give our house a little character. Thus, we added "them fancy doors" and a few other amenities. We were on a perpetual search for bargains. We located a wallpaper store in a town called Toto where the wallpaper sold for one dollar a double roll. Toto was even smaller than Preston. It had one four-way stop. I once jokingly commented on the name of the town, saying it was named after Dorothy's dog.

"Oh, no. That ain't right," said one of the locals. "Dorothy's dog was named after Toto! Frank Baum used to spend his summers near here and he used our town name in The Wizard of Oz!"

On our sales trips we were always on the lookout for materials for the house. We were at a point where we could think about purchasing carpeting when we passed a carpet store in a tiny town in northwest Indiana. This town was almost nonexistent, it was so small.

However, it did have a concrete block building which said "Carpet" on it. We had a little extra time, so we stopped and went in. The store was a cavernous room full of rolls of ugly carpet that must have been rejected by every buyer in northern Indiana. In the center of the room was an open office area with a cash register and a phone. The door to the building was wide open, but there was no one inside. The merchandise was safe...no one would have stolen that carpet. Carsten wandered around, hoping to find a bargain, while I stood near the front desk, looking for a clerk. That's when I spotted the sign. It was carefully hand-lettered on a large piece of cardboard:

INSTRUCTIONS FOR LAYING CARPET
1. Remove all furniture from room
2. Remove old carpet
3. Ask clerk for further instructions

We never did find the clerk, but we did not need any help because the carpet was not to our taste. The sign, however, provided us with many laughs.

"Can't you see it?" Carsten said. "Someone would forget to follow those instructions and they would say, 'Didn't we used to have a piano? And what is that large lump in the corner?' "

"And where's the baby?" I added.

I discovered I could do a pretty good job of laying ceramic tile and I tiled the walls of the new downstairs bathroom. It was so beautiful I couldn't stop until I had tiled twice as much of the room as I had originally intended. I also tiled the floor of the front foyer, around where the living room wood stove was to go and the entire area off of the living room where my piano would be placed. My hands were raw from the adhesive and grout. My elbow rebelled from cutting tiles and at times I couldn't even pick up a glass of water. We found parquet flooring at a store that was going out of business and Carsten laid it in the dining room. I learned to cut miters for the trim around the ceiling and floors and around the windows.

The new living room had two large bookcases. Carsten previously worked for a large publishing house in New York. One of the perks of his job was to take one book home with him every week. He built up an impressive library this way and we now had shelves for all of them.

Carsten put the exterior wood siding on the house. In between bouts of temper and verbal outbursts, he sided the entire house..... old part and new addition. It was my job to stain it. The front porch on the old part needed attention. The pillars filled with bird nests had to go. While traveling, we saw an old house being demolished. It had beautiful pillars and we asked if we could buy them. We ended up with lovely fluted pillars covered with about eight layers of paint, which had to be removed before we repainted. We took down the old pillars and found that the birds had made their nests in there every year, one on top of the other, for about twenty years. For years after we replaced the pillars, the birds returned and dive-bombed us for destroying their home.

We spent many hours in hardware stores, lumberyards and paint stores. While waiting for service at a lumberyard, we over-heard the following conversation between a sales clerk and a cus-tomer.

Customer: "Do you have any copper screening?"

Clerk: "Nope, but this here aluminum screen works just as good."

Customer: "Well, I'm working on a Frank Lloyd Wright house and I need copper."

Clerk: "Hey, just take this aluminum screen. Frank won't mind."

After many years, the house was useable, but never completed. The stairs were just sub floor and had "Kiln Dried Wood" stamped on them. The upstairs hallway was also sub flooring. Many doors did not have doorknobs. The living room was bricked half way up the wall behind the wood stove, but we never had a mantle. We still had to fix up parts of the old house and we put a new ceiling and walls in the bedroom off the kitchen.

We moved into the new part and were happy to have the room. However, all did not work as planned: the roof leaked where the two houses met; the pipes for the hot water heat sometimes froze and burst; and the heating system had to be supplemented by wood burning stoves in the kitchen, living room, and basement. A large supply of wood, which we gathered from our forest, was required to keep the wood stoves filled. Because we never had enough wood to get us through the winter, we spent many cold and snowy days riding out on the antique Farmall tractor with an old cart behind, to gather more wood. Carsten cut the dead trees down with his chain saw. As he cut the trees into smaller pieces, I threw them into the cart. We then hauled the load back to the house, unloaded the cart, and Carsten split the wood. We stacked some of the wood on the porch and the rest in the yard. Keeping the wood stacked on the porch and keeping the fires going required constant attention. I discovered wood does terrible things to your hands and every winter my hands were dry, red and peeling unless I remembered to wear work gloves when I handled it.

The water pressure was still low, so we installed a special shower head in the upstairs bathroom. Carsten, who had just finished installing all of the plumbing, decided to try it out. While in the shower, he began to yell about the continued lack of water pressure. I reached in and turned the shower head until a decent stream of water was produced.

"How did you do that?" Carsten asked.

It was the small things he couldn't handle.

People make a lot of a house. They think of it as a statement of themselves….of their likes, dislikes, tastes and feelings. They use their house as a display of their wealth and success. They speak lovingly of making a house a home.

Our house did none of that for me. It consumed me. It filled every moment I wasn't working for our business. Build it, paint it, decorate it, clean it, heat it, cool it. No warm glow filled my soul when I drove up the long, muddy driveway. Instead, I felt nausea, dread and fatigue. This house depleted us both and yet it was never a thing to admire or a place of beauty. It never produced a sense of satisfaction. Often, when I felt overwhelmed by it all, I would quote Goldye Hawn, who said, in the movie *Private Benjamin*, "I want to be normal again! I want to go to lunch!"

Ralph Waldo Emerson seemed to have my same feelings about houses when he said, "A man builds a fine house; and now he has a master, and a task for life: he is to furnish, watch, show it and keep it in repair, the rest of his days." I did not have a fine house, but I certainly had a master.

THE TOWN BY THE TRACKS

The gathering of houses called Preston was a short distance down the road from our farm. The latest census report said 200 people lived there, but Carsten said they must have counted the dogs.

My presence in Preston, along with Dan and Amy, my two children still with me, increased the population by 1.5 per cent. Carsten's two boys, who lived about 35 miles away and seldom visited, didn't count. Amy went away to prep school, thanks to the generosity of her grandmother, and Dan, who was one year older, elected to go to high school in Indiana. There was no high school in Preston, so he rode the bus about eight miles each way to school.

Preston had its beginnings as a small railroad community. It had been platted in the 1850s and incorporated in the 1870s because of a feud between the townspeople and the township. The feud was so bitter that no resident of the town could be elected to a township office. By incorporating, they could elect a Justice of the Peace. After a few years, tempers cooled and Preston then unincorporated. It had remained that way ever since.

The railroad track still ran past our farm and through the town. The train used to stop in Preston, because there were businesses of the kind found in most villages of the nineteenth century: two hotels, a hardware store and a lumberyard. Now, all that remained was the depot, which was moved a block away from the tracks and made into a house.

When I arrived in the early 1980s, Preston had a few nice houses, interspersed with trailers and asphalt-shingled shacks. Traffic was regulated by one four-way stop sign.

A general store, which had a gas pump in the front and a video store in the back, was in the center of town. Most of the food in the store dated back two or three years. Carsten delighted in asking Gary, the store owner, if the lobster bisque had arrived yet. A string of colored Christmas tree lights encircled the roof of the store. They remained there all year around and were turned on at Christmas time. I was told the building had once housed a bank. Now the closest bank was eight miles away.

A filling station/garage was run by a fellow we called Dirty Del, an amorphous lump of a man in his early 60s. He worked in Bradford, the nearest "real" town, as the night janitor of a small factory and he ran his garage during the day. His crew cut was a holdover from Preston High School days and his fingernails had never met a nail brush. He competed with Gary's general store for gas sales and regulated his prices by always being one cent cheaper. The business office was covered with a thick layer of dust, proof that nothing had ever been sold there.

The garage where Dirty Del tried to repair cars was in the back. On the rare occasion when someone brought in a car for Del to fix, he would call the automobile factory and pretend he was the owner of the car and needed to know how to repair it. They would tell him what to do and he would try to follow their instructions. More often than not, he got it wrong.

Del's garage also served as a meeting place for the retired men of the community. They sat on car seats, which had been removed from junk cars, around a large stove in which Del burned old tires for warmth.

Del's father was in his 90s and sometimes joined the group. He lived a few miles outside of town and still drove. His eyes weren't too good anymore and he once went off the side of the road into a culvert. After that incident, he avoided the problem by driving down the middle of the road. Everyone in town recognized his car and just pulled over when they saw him coming.

The post office was in the remodeled garage of the local manic-depressive postmaster, who played religious music on the radio all day. There was no house-to-house mail delivery and residents had to retrieve their mail from a box at the post office. Separation of church and state notwithstanding, they simultaneously got their mail and a healthy dose of fundamentalist Christianity.

The constant barrage of religion didn't uplift our postmaster—-quite the opposite. He was dark and moody and often would not talk for days. I made it my mission to get him to smile or talk, and babbled inanities to him every time I went to the post office. I pretended I was delighted to see him...that my visit to the post office was the highlight of my day. I tried to guess how long it would take for him to speak to me. Sometimes it took 4 or 5 days.

The town once had a K-12 school. The old school, which was built in 1902 and closed in 1973, was partially standing, surrounded by rubble. Many years before I came, a man had been hired to demolish the building, but the money ran out and so did he. Bricks and timbers were left strewn across the school yard, a sad monument to what used to be the mainstay of the town.

From the local residents, I got an idea of what the school must have meant to them. Because everyone knew each other, the children could not get away with any nonsense. The parents were immediately notified of all transgressions. Some children came to school so dirty that the staff washed their clothes and gave them baths. The consolidated school that followed may have brought them better educational facilities, but a vital part of the community was now gone.

With the loss of the school, the Preston Methodist Church became the only remaining institution. It had a small, but loyal, congregation.

Preston had two social organizations. One was the I.O.O.F.-The International Order of Odd Fellows. Membership was by invitation, and Carsten was never invited to join, a social slight that was the cause of much teasing by both his family and mine. We all thought he should be at least an honorary member, because he was a very odd fellow.

The other group was the volunteer firemen. On weekends they would gather at the fire station and get out the big trucks so they could rev the engines and flex their muscles. They had a yearly fish fry to raise money. Everyone pooled the excess fish they had caught and frozen over the past year and hosted a big dinner, which was served in the firehouse. The firehouse had no ventilation except from the two large garage doors which were opened wide to let air and people in.

The uninvited guests were the flies. Thousands of flies. We had to eat with one hand and wave our napkins with the other. After just one of these dinners, we got take-out, forgoing the biggest social event of the year.

Carsten found a description of flies eating, which said:

This is what happens
when a fly lands on your food.
Flies can't eat solid food,
so to soften it up they vomit on it.
Then they stamp the vomit in
until it's a liquid, usually stamping in
a few germs for good measure.
Then when it's good and runny
they suck it all back again, probably
dropping some excrement at the same time.
And then, when they've finished eating,
it's your turn.

He wanted to hang it on the wall at the next fish fry, but thought better of it when I reminded him these were volunteer firemen and we might need them sometime.

Most of the area around the town was farmland. The locals grew meager crops on the sandy soil. There were also dairy, hog and sheep farms. Many farms had tall blue silos equipped with stars on top which were lit during the Christmas season.

A small, rectangular park with a picnic table, swings and a black asphalt tennis court was located beside the fire station. We were the only ones in town who owned tennis racquets, so I can't explain how the court came to be there. Whenever we tried to play there, the neighboring farmer decided to fertilize his field, bringing our game to an abrupt halt.

A lamp shop was in one couple's garage and across the street was a beauty parlor. An empty building across from the general store housed different businesses at different times, with an average life span of six months.

ॐॐ

At a short distance to the west of town stood a box of a house that always struck me as curious. I don't think the town had any boundaries, but this house was neither close enough to be considered a part of it nor far enough away not to be. It was covered with asphalt shingles made to look like brick and sat on a corner lot. The grass on the lawn was always weedless and perfectly mowed. The odd thing was that not a tree, not a bush, not a flower was on the entire lot. The only thing I ever saw in the yard was a large trampoline.

One day, I drove by the property and nothing was there. The lot was totally bare. All evidence of the house was gone. The next time I drove by, a large metal pole building stood where the house had been. The south side of the building was made of some sort of translucent material. I assumed it was being used by a farmer for his equipment.

Several months later, I noticed a big sign in the yard: "Garage Sale."

The large doors on the west end were ajar and I could see many items for sale on that side of the building. As I contemplated what exactly the building was being used for, I noticed something behind the garage sale items: a house trailer. The owners were living in a trailer encased by a large building. I could see how this arrangement could have its advantages. They never had to worry about rain, the translucent panels admitted light, and, best of all, they could have their garage sale all year long.

I liked to talk to Gary at the general store, because he knew everything that was going on.

"Hey, Gary," I said one day. "What's with the house down at the corner that disappeared one day and now there's an aluminum shed there with a trailer inside?"

"A guy lives there with his family. Guess he thought that was the easiest way to live. I really don't know him, but I hear he has a pipe organ in there. Brought it over from Europe, I think."

"Very funny," I said. "Now what's the real story?"

"Not kidding," Gary said. "I've never seen it, but that's what I heard."

As the months passed, I hardly noticed the strange building anymore, until one Memorial Day weekend. Amy, my youngest, was home from graduate school. My niece, Jennifer, and her husband Chris, came over from Chicago. Before Jennifer married Chris, she lived in a shotgun apartment in the heart of Chicago. She was never afraid when she lived there, but when she visited us on the farm, she could hardly sleep at night because she was so scared. Now that she had Chris, she felt much safer.

We planned a fun time on the farm, fishing, playing croquet, cooking out and riding around on Carsten's 50-year-old tractor. And then it rained. It rained on Friday, again on Saturday, and even a little on Sunday morning. Jennifer was able to put her entire fist in her mouth and Amy could recite the whole alphabet during one long belch, but practicing these feats did not entertain us for long and we soon grew bored. After eating our way through Friday night and Saturday, we decided we had to think of something. I mentioned we had a camcorder and suggested making a travel video for my son, Dan, who was now in the Navy. We could say it was created by the Preston Travel and Tourism Commission and we could include all of the points of interest. The idea was greeted with enthusiasm.

Starting with our own house, which was constantly under construction, and the unfinished barn, we embarked on our tour. We drove down the dirt driveway in Jennifer and Chris's new van. We filmed the apartments, looking sorry and wet. Next was our closest neighbor, Maxine Marlowe, cleaning up after her daughter's graduation party and then a house with a large solar panel like the one on Carsten's barn. They had gotten the idea from him. In their yard, was a car with a totally flattened top. Their daughter had rolled it recently. Fortunately, she wasn't hurt, but the car was left there as a reminder, I suppose.

Next was a house with peeling paint and a few broken windows, which belonged to a large family named Babcock. I would get to know them well in the coming years.

Then came a pleasant little stretch of road that could have been Anycountrytown, USA. Five houses in a row were neat and shaded. The road ran into Central Street, the town's main thoroughfare. Central Street went past the grocery/filling station/video store, the church, what was once the school, the beauty parlor, the lamp shop, the fire department and the park. It had a four-way stop sign and went over the railroad track. We had great fun naming all of the local sites: the store became the Preston Mall and we dubbed the half demolished school The Preston War Memorial.... it was, after all, Memorial Day. The International Order of Odd Fellows became the University Club and the worst house in town, we decided, was the Bed and Breakfast.

We passed the cemetery, which was one of the loveliest places in Preston. It was on a small hill and had beautiful old oaks and maples. Next to the cemetery was a little house snuggled into a copse of trees and surrounded by beautiful flowers. It could have been a doll house, it looked so neat and small.

Splashing through puddles along the tarred roads, we passed the foam house, our favorite tourist site. This house was completely covered with mustard yellow foam insulation. Windows and doors showed as indentations in the foam. The word "foam" was written...in foam...across the front.

Our next scene was a large wooden sign about five feet high and six feet across in the front yard of a farm house. It read:

Hey, Walter (Cowboy) Jones
Where's my $325?
May,1988

We decided this should be the local savings and loan.

We continued on to one of the newest and largest homes in the area. Two small ponds connected by an arched bridge were in the front yard. A miniature lighthouse stood in one pond along with a sign that said "Lake Dinky Little". Everything was painted light blue. Ducks and geese swam in the ponds. The owners had a parking lot in the rear of the house with actual parking meters and authentic looking street signs with their children's names on them.

On our way home, we passed the metal building with the trailer inside. The "Garage Sale" sign attracted Jennifer and, having nothing better to do, we pulled over and went inside. Shelves around the walls and tables on the floor were filled with plastic flowers, outdated appliances and used clothing. Of the most interest to Jennifer was a basket of kittens. Her husband, who abided cats only because he loved Jennifer, kept the camcorder running.

The resident, alerted to a possible sale, came from the inside trailer to the outside building. He was a jovial fellow in his 60s, who stood and watched us while we pretended to be interested in his sale items. I'm not good at making small talk with strangers, but I did my best with him, hoping the conversation would lead to organs, or music, or pipes. I knew I couldn't pass up this opportunity. I got nowhere with my plan, so I just blurted it out.

"I hear you have a pipe organ in here."

His answer was guarded. "Where did you hear that?"

"It's just something I heard around town."

He paused, pushing his glasses up on his nose while looking me over. Obviously, he was uncertain about what to tell me. After what seemed to be a very long time, he said, "Would you like to see it?"

Of course I would! I signaled to the others and we entered the inner sanctum of the doublewide trailer. The windowless living room was long and narrow. A couch with many pillows at one end was along one wall. "I got something wrong with me. Got to lie with my feet elevated most of the time," our host explained.

Two television sets airing different baseball games stood against the opposite wall.

We never exchanged names. He seemed uninterested in knowing who we were and I was so curious about the organ that my curiosity took precedence over my manners.

Then I saw it. At the end of the room was a large organ. It was not a pipe organ from Europe, as Gary had described. It was a theater organ. The owner turned off the room lights and flipped a switch on the organ. It came to life. Lights flickered and blinked and then stayed ablaze. It had four rows of keys. Above the keys was a semicircle of colored levers. They were green, yellow, red, blue, black and white. We gazed at it in amazement.

Once reluctant, our host was now anxious to tell us all about it. "The organ was made for silent movies. It was on a lift that took it down in a pit. All four keyboards have the same notes on them. They just have different sounds on each keyboard. Different instruments play on different keyboards."

"Where did you get this?" I asked.

"Kokomo. But it was originally in a movie house in Chicago. It was built in 1927. I heard it was for sale and I went down there to look at it. I got two daughters and I never gave them anything but what was educational. We never gave them no cards or games. I saw this and thought it would be somethin' they could learn, so I took it all apart and brung it up here."

Jennifer was amazed. "You took it apart and put it back together?"

"Yep. Couldn't move it no other way." He leaned over and flipped another switch. A large blowing sound started and the entire trailer began to vibrate.

"That's the blower," he explained. "You can play it now."

"Would you play it for us?" Amy asked.

He laughed. "I can't play! I can't play a note!"

"You put this entire thing together and you can't play a note?" I asked.

"That's right. I got this for my girls."

That being the case, Amy and I started picking out tunes on it while he punched buttons to make train whistles, bird cheeps, chimes and tambourine sounds.

"The pedals play notes, too," our host explained.

Amy and I tried to play the Navy hymn.

"We're making a video for my son, who is in the Navy," I told him. "That's why I'm trying to play Navy songs."

"My uncle was a lieutenant commander in the Navy," he said. He reached down beside the organ and produced a book of Navy songs.

"Oh, how perfect!" Amy said.

"Can you read music?" he asked.

"Yes," we replied in unison.

He seemed amazed. "You can?"

Amy and I found "God Bless My Boy At Sea" in the book and tried to play it.

Chris was getting tired of listening to us and wanted to get on with his movie making. "Where are the pipes?" he asked.

That was the key question. How could all of those pipes fit into a trailer? We were soon to find out.

"They's out there," he said, pointing to a side door. "This here's nothing but switches and wires."

He led us through the door. Here were pipes as far as we could see. Row after row of huge pipes, tiny pipes and every size in between were nestled between the outer building and the inner building. Most were metal pipes but some were wooden. There were drums, tambourines, cymbals, castanets and maracas...all parts of the enormous organ. A train whistle tooted from high up on the wall and a bird whistle chirped beside me. An entire xylophone stood vertically under the percussion instruments. The words "MAKE IN CHINA" were printed on a drum.

"Here's the directions they gave me to put it back together," he said, pointing to a 4 by 8 inch card tacked to the wall.

"That was all you had?" Amy asked. "How long did it take you to put it together?"

"I ain't done yet. See those pipes lyin' down in the back?"

We peered through the darkness and could see huge pipes, larger than we were, lying on their sides. Chris kept the camera going. No one would believe this unless it was captured on tape.

When we returned to the living room, one of our host's daughters was there. She was an attractive girl in her twenties. She explained that she no longer lived at home, but had just come by for a visit. After introducing ourselves, we asked her if she could play the organ.

"I took lessons," she said.

"Play something for them," her proud father said.

She self-consciously sat at the organ and, reading from sheet music, began to play. We stood and listened in quiet wonder. She did not play a beautiful melody or a piece that might have been the background for a silent movie love story or melodrama. Instead, she haltingly played "The Gambler" by Kenny Rogers. If Kenny had been there and had tried to sing along with her, it would have gone something like this:

Yougot taknowwhen to hold
em yougotta know when tofold em you
gotta know when to walk awayandknow whentorun
You gottacount your mon eywhenyou're sit-in' atthetable
There'llbe timeenoughfor count in'when the deal in'sdone.

It was painful to listen to and we were grateful when she finally finished. We then said our thank-yous and made a hasty retreat.

Thus ended our tour and our video. The video became an invaluable tool for describing our lifestyle to my city friends. After listening to the rendition of "The Gambler", not a single one of them has been able to identify the song.

LOVE THY NEIGHBOR

My first encounter with the local residents occurred one evening shortly after we married. A strange looking couple arrived at our kitchen door just as we were finishing dinner. They seemed to be quite familiar with Carsten and he invited them in while we finished eating.

Carsten introduced them to me as Robert and Candy Babcock. They were a young couple in their mid to late thirties. Robert stood about six feet tall. A shock of dirty brown hair stuck out from under an even dirtier red baseball cap. He wore soiled blue coveralls and his boots were covered with mud. His brown eyes had a wild, feral look to them, as if he were eluding the law or on the edge of madness. Candy, who was much shorter than her husband, had a thin face, a round lumpy body and wide hips. She had a huge belly, which she accommodated by wearing a pair of what were probably Robert's bib overalls, cut off to make the legs shorter. A wool knit cap was pulled down to her eyebrows and wisps of greasy hair fringed her face.

"Please, have a seat," I said.

"Nope, we're O.K.," replied Robert, looking around in amazement at our house, which was now furnished with my possessions. They were a big improvement over the previous furnishings, which had been returned to the Salvation Army.

The Babcocks stood by the table and watched us finish eating. I kept trying to send eye signals to Carsten, indicating he should insist they sit down, but he ignored me. When we finished, I cleared the table as they continued standing.

"We been fishin' in your pond," Robert said. "We didn't catch nothin', but you're always lettin' us fish, so we wanted to bring you this as a kind of thank you."

He handed Carsten a package wrapped in butcher paper and string.

"What is it?" Carsten asked.

"Ven-e-son. You know, deer meat."

"Where did you get this? It's hardly deer season," Carsten said, as he hesitantly took the package from Robert.

"Out on the highway," Robert answered. "Hit by an eighteen-wheeler."

Candy spoke for the first time. "Robert's brother called early yesterday morning and told us about it. We was out there before the carcass was cold. Got it skinned and hung that same morning," she said proudly. She looked at Robert and smiled at her great provider.

"I don't know what I'd call the cut I gave you," Candy continued. "It was pretty banged up and I couldn't git the pieces cut like normal."

I couldn't touch it. "Put it in the freezer," I told Carsten. "I wouldn't want it to spoil. "

Roadkill was a poor substitute for the baskets of goodies delivered by Welcome Wagon in Springfield.

"Won't you sit down?" I asked Robert and Candy again.

"Well, don't mind if I do," Robert replied, while pulling out a kitchen chair. He sat down on his tailbone, his long legs sprawling under the table and coming out the other side. Candy sat down too, rather daintily considering her bulk.

Robert and Carsten struck up a conversation about fishing. I am not a fisherman, nor do I ever intend to be one, but I feigned interest because I couldn't think of a thing to say to Candy. I sat silently for a while and then decided nothing could be worse than the fish conversation. Turning to Candy, I said, "Where do you live?"

"Right down the road a piece."

"Do you have any children?"

"Four," she replied proudly. "They's twelve, eleven, six and four."

"And where are they now?" I wondered aloud.

"Home. They's good kids and are real responsible. They know where we're at."

We chatted about nothing in particular until Robert rose from his seat and Candy obediently followed him out into the night.

I turned to Carsten for an explanation. "Are they friends of yours?"

"They're neighbors," he said, "and I let them fish in the pond because they have a lot of mouths to feed and not much money."

"And why did they stand there and watch us eat?" I continued.

"I don't know why, but it seems to be the custom around here. Everyone always stands and watches you eat," he explained.

I got a broom and began sweeping up the pile of dirt that had fallen off of Robert's shoes. As I swept, I pressed Carsten for more information about the Babcocks.

"They live in that little house down the road….you know, the one on the curve. Robert works in a small factory. They have lots of kids and some horses. They kind of live off the land."

"And the highway," I said.

A few weeks later, while we were standing in our yard, a rusty pickup truck sped up our driveway. Robert excitedly jumped out of the truck while it was still running.

"Candy had twins last night!" he shouted. "A boy and a girl."

I now realized why Candy looked so strange and lumpy.

Carsten seemed truly happy for Robert. He grabbed his dirty hand and pumped it enthusiastically. "Are they identical?" he asked.

"Don't know fer sure," Robert answered.

I stood by speechlessly and then went inside to see if I could find a physiology book to show both of them.

I thought it would be nice to take gifts to their new babies. After all, they had given us some roadkill. I bought two sleeper suits, carefully wrapped them, and took them down to the Babcocks. They lived in a small, decrepit, paint-deprived house about four doors down toward town. A rusted swing set with no swings sat in the side yard. A few tufts of grass were struggling to survive in the barren lawn. Various homemade animal pens were behind the house. One held a large rabbit and another held a beagle with faded black and brown spots. The rest of the pens were empty.

Because I was unable to locate a front door, I went around to the back. The original back door had been replaced with an interior French door. It was missing several panes of glass. Most of the door was covered with mud. I knocked on one small, mudless spot.

Candy answered the door with one baby slung over her arm. She was surprisingly chipper and rested for someone who had recently given birth to twins. Her body, though still without much form, was considerably smaller than when I had last seen her.

"Come in, come in," she said, opening the door with her free arm.

I entered the kitchen and stood looking around me, just like Candy and Robert had stood in our kitchen. Candy invited me to sit, although she did not indicate where, and I warily eyed the possible places. The table was covered with a thin film of jelly. The metal kitchen chairs had padded vinyl seats that were split with cotton stuffing protruding from them. Blobs of peanut butter were on the backs of some of the chairs. I pulled out a chair that was not as bad as the others and gingerly sat down, careful not to touch the sticky table.

The second twin was in a baby seat on the floor. The floor was linoleum, vintage 1950, and worn through to the floor boards in the most heavily trafficked areas. Hand prints decorated the kitchen walls, which had evidently been painted yellow at one time. The kitchen sink was full of dirty dishes. A gas hot water heater, with the gas flame clearly exposed, sputtered in one corner. A wood stove stood in another corner. Streaks of creosote, a highly flammable resin, ran down the stovepipe. I had enough experience with wood stoves to recognize this as evidence they were burning soft pine and green wood, creating a real fire hazard. The stovepipe went through the roof with no insulation around it. It was an accident waiting to happen. Various children ran in and out of the room. In addition to the twins, there were three girls and a boy. A black cocker spaniel was nursing a litter of puppies under the table.

I placed the presents in my lap so they wouldn't get dirty. I tried to admire the twins but declined the invitation to hold one. They already had what I referred to as the Preston pallor. As the other children scampered in and out of the kitchen, I noticed they, too, had a "Coca Cola for breakfast" look to their complexions. Their skin lacked the glow and rosiness of better-nourished children, their eyes and hair were dull and lifeless.

Vachel Lindsay, Springfield's own poet, seemed to be describing these very children in his poem, "The Leaden-Eyed", when he wrote:

It is the world's one crime its babes grow dull,
Its poor are ox-like, limp and leaden-eyed.

I remembered the bottles I had sterilized, the diapers I had bleached, the sweet little outfits I had washed and ironed, the playpens and toys I had scrubbed, and realized here was a true test of Darwin's survival of the fittest. These children were probably healthier than mine, who had suffered from all of the prevalent childhood diseases in spite of my efforts. These children were exposed to germs early in life and their little bodies learned to fight them off. They would probably grow up stronger because of it.

I finally remembered what I was there for and handed Candy the packages. She opened them and held the sleepers up to the little twins. She was very gracious and thanked me politely.

I stayed as long as I could stand it, then made my apologies for the brevity of my visit and left. This all happened before we remodeled our house and, when I entered our kitchen, I smiled as I gazed around at the slightly worn floor, the strange red kitchen cabinets, the ugly yellow counter tops and the pile of mail on the kitchen table. It looked beautiful.

Candy was a horse lover. She could throw her leg across the back of a horse and ride it as if she had been born there. She actually looked graceful when she was astride a galloping horse.

Robert also liked horses, but I suspected his interest was just a result of living with Candy. He believed himself to be a horse trainer and someone entrusted a horse to Robert to break. Because our place had more acreage and was quieter than his, he kept the horse on our farm. After a few days of working with it, Robert came to our door and asked to see Carsten. His eyes looked wilder than usual and he was noticeably frightened.

"Can I put this horse in your woods?" he asked, when Carsten came outside.

"Why do you want to do that?" Carsten asked.

"I was havin' trouble with the damn horse and just lost my temper," Robert said.

"And?" Carsten said.

"And I hit him in the head with a board. Now his eye don't look too good, like it's gonna pop out or sumthin'. The owner wants to come pay a visit and see how he's doin' and I'm gonna tell him I took him out to another farm a few miles away and I'll bring him back next week."

Carsten, the pushover, agreed, and Robert took the poor creature and tied him to a tree in the woods. Robert's evasion tactic worked and the owner was none the wiser when the horse was returned to him, but I let Carsten know I never again wanted to let Robert "board" horses on our farm.

Late one night, I was awakened by a strange noise outside. It was followed by loud, impatient knocking on the kitchen door.

Carsten was still downstairs and I heard him open the door.

"Oh, he's beautiful, Robert." I heard him say. "Where did you get him?"

I tried to hear the rest of the conversation, but it was too muffled to understand. Robert was slurring his words and I only caught snippets of his conversation. His voice was sometimes loud and raucous—sometimes soft and blurred. I heard him mention cards and winning. He sounded excited and I thought I heard snorting. When I heard him leave, I ventured downstairs.

"What did he want?" I asked Carsten. "He sounded drunk."

"Yeah, he was a little drunk. He just won a horse in a card game and wondered if he could keep it here."

"A horse in a card game! I never heard of such a thing! Why did he think we could keep it here? We have no barn or anything."

"We have a fenced pasture," Carsten replied. "I told him we would be glad to keep it."

I sighed. Sometimes Carsten's generosity overwhelmed me. "You did this after our last experience with Robert and a horse? And what will our responsibilities be? Will we be expected to feed and water it? What will we do in the winter, or when it rains?"

"He promised to take good care of it. We won't have to do a thing. And people around here leave their animals outside all year around. They don't worry about the weather."

I tried to be positive. "I guess it will keep the grass cut for us," I said.

"That's my girl," Carsten said, giving me a hug. "You are finally coming around. I'll make a country girl out of you yet."

Robert came back the next day to admire his new acquisition.

The horse was a beautiful animal.

"What are you going to call him, Robert?" Carsten asked.

"I decided to call him Con," Robert answered.

Carsten thought the name was curious. "Why are you calling him Con?"

"I named him after the big one. You know........King Con." Robert replied.

Con stayed in our field, happily munching apples and grass. I had to admit the pasture had never looked so good. Con was soon joined by Candy's mare Lady who, shortly thereafter, had a colt. Candy and Robert brought a battered, claw-foot bathtub for a watering trough and placed it in the pasture, expecting it would be kept full with rainwater. This did not happen, and the task of filling the tub fell to me. On the rare occasions the Babcocks brought food for them, Lady would kick and bite her colt so she could get to it first.

A dirty, scruffy pony joined Con and Lady a few months after the colt was born. They named the pony Beauty and explained that she belonged to their daughters. They continued to ignore the horses and fed and watered them only when the mood struck.

"The horses are hungry," I told Carsten. "When I drive up the driveway, they run to the fence and whinny."

"Why don't you go down and tell the Babcocks?" Carsten replied. It was 10 a.m., and he was sitting at the kitchen table in his nightshirt. Because he worked out of our house and didn't like to get up early, he often did not get dressed until around noon. The morning chores of fixing breakfast, getting the mail, answering the phone, and cleaning the kitchen fell to me.

"Have you gotten the mail yet?" Carsten asked.

"No."

"Well then, you have to pass right by their house. Just stop in and tell them to get up here and feed the horses."

I reluctantly consented.

"What kin I do fer you?" Candy asked when she answered her door.

"It's the horses," I said. "They're hungry and need some hay. I also wish you could keep the tub full of water. I just don't have time to do that."

"That ain't no trouble. Jist git a hose and fill it." Candy appeared surprised that I did not want to perform the simple chore.

"Our hose seems to have disappeared," I replied.

"Well, I'll tell Robert and he'll take care of it," Candy said as she closed the door in my face.

That evening, Robert drove up our driveway in his battered truck. In the back of the truck was an enormous roll of hay. I watched as he drove into the pasture and hopped out. With great difficulty and the aid of a long pole, he rolled the hay into the middle of the pasture. Without ever looking at the horses, he drove away.

That is when I learned about the eating habits of horses. They will eat as long as there is food in front of them. Con, Beauty, Lady and her colt began to eat and did not move from the roll of hay. The next morning, I looked outside and Beauty was still eating. Her sides were so swollen she looked pregnant with triplets. When she finally stopped eating, she staggered so much she nearly fell over. Later I learned that horses cannot vomit and when they get a stomach ache, they have to be walked and sometimes seen by a vet, because they could die. The vet has to perform a procedure that entails the use of a very long rubber glove. Miraculously, Beauty didn't die that day.

The horse situation only got worse. In the winter, they stood shivering in the rain and snow. Carsten sometimes had to lift great sheets of ice off their backs. After two years, I begged Carsten to speak to the Babcocks about taking the horses to their house. He refused. He didn't seem bothered by the horses. When Candy and Robert came to the farm, he was always cordial and jovial. I, on the other hand, could not disguise my feelings and would often retreat to the house in order not to lash out at them.

One day I took matters into my own hands. Without telling Carsten, I went to the Babcock's. I was invited in, but not offered a seat.

"I'm going to have to ask you to take the horses," I said. "They've gotten to be too much trouble. Also, I'm trying to paint the outside of the house, and the flies keep getting into the paint. I'm sorry, but we just can't keep them any longer."

Robert glared at me. "Horses don't draw flies," he said.

I wanted to yell, "The hell they don't!" but I held my tongue. Robert was starting to get a wild look in his eyes that frightened me.

"That's O.K.," Candy said. "We'll keep 'em up here."

I don't know why, but I apologized for making trouble.

"Don't you fret," Candy said. "We'll git 'em tonight."

I left without saying good-bye. I just wanted out of their house. Something was simmering on the stove and it was making me nauseous. As I stood outside the door, breathing in the fresh spring air, I heard Robert say, "Too bad Carsten had to up and marry her. Things was better before she came."

That night Robert came and got Con and the two older girls got Beauty and the mare. Candy arrived in their old sedan with the back seat removed and we watched in amazement as she led the colt up to the car and pushed it into the back. After she got it situated, with its head out of the left window and its tail out of the right, Candy hopped into the car and drove home as if it were the normal way to transport horses.

Our horse boarding did not end then. Off and on through the years, the horses were brought back, because the bill collectors were coming or the bank was threatening to foreclose and Candy and Robert didn't want anyone to know they had horses, for fear they might have to sell them.

All of the children in the Babcock family learned to ride horses when they were very young. The twins were five years old when Robert and Candy started teaching them the art of equestrianism. I did not have the pleasure of watching, but our closest neighbors, the Marlowes, described a disturbing scene.

"Robert placed the boy twin on Lady and began leading them around. Things were going fine until the horse was spooked by a flapping shirt on the clothesline. She bucked and the twin fell off, injuring himself only slightly. Robert was furious. He got his old rusty truck and tied the horse to it. He then drove the truck up and down the road, making Lady run behind until she nearly dropped from exhaustion."

"Oh, my God," I said. "Can't we do something about their treatment of animals?"

"We were tempted to call the Humane Society, but we didn't," Maxine Marlowe said. "Robert was proud of his parenting skills and his display of manliness that proved he was in charge. It almost made me sick."

One lovely spring day, Robert came bumping up our driveway in an Amish carriage pulled by Con. Robert was quite excited and, temporarily ignoring his dislike for me, invited me to go for a ride with him. The carriage had once belonged to a large Amish family and it was quite old and close to the end of its useful life. I accepted Robert's offer, climbed up into the battered carriage and seated myself on the cracked leather seat. Con stepped lively and looked quite handsome as he trotted along. Robert, the entrepreneur, smiled at me, exposing his yellow, rotting teeth.

"I'll rent it out for weddin's and I'll dress up in a top hat and fancy clothes and drive the bride and groom around," he said. I conjured up visions of a lovely bride and handsome groom in this sorry carriage with its odd driver. I do not think he ever got his new enterprise started.

The Babcock's fourth child, the youngest before the twins were born, was named Robert junior, but was called Bertie. I struck up a friendship with him because, in spite of being somewhat ignored and neglected by his parents, he was a cheerful little fellow. He was always willing to work hard and I became quite fond of him. The Babcock's home was deprived of the basic childhood toys, games, books and art materials, so Bertie was thrilled when I gave him crayons and watercolors. He enjoyed watching our educational filmstrips and videos and looking at picture books. He often stayed at our house too long and, because their telephone was usually disconnected by the phone company, Candy never called him home. My son, Dan, was there one day when I suggested he give Bertie a ride home. Dan thought of every excuse except imminent sniper attacks for not taking him home.

I finally sent Bertie away on foot and turned to Dan.

"Why wouldn't you take him home? He had been here long enough and you are always anxious for him to go."

"I didn't want him in my car."

"Why not?"

"Because he smells bad and I didn't want him to stink up my car," Dan said.

The smell was a problem with Bertie, but I somehow got used to it. His visits became quite frequent. If I had work to do on the house, he was content to pound nails into an old board. If I was outside, he gladly hoed in the garden, something he had learned to do at home, as the Babcocks grew much of their own food. Bertie was a little slow and I suspected he was in special education classes at school. His questions betrayed the limits of his experiences.

"What are those?" he asked, when I put place mats on the table. He told me he didn't own a toothbrush.

Bill Burns, the minister of the Methodist church, expressed his concerns about Bertie on a rare occasion when he attended Sunday School.

"He had his coat on upside down!" Bill said.

"What do you mean?" I asked. "Inside out? Backwards?"

"No," Bill replied. "It was upside down. The collar was down around his knees. I've never seen anyone do that before."

Bertie came to the house one day to tell me of a new acquisition.

"We have a new cow," he said.

"You do?" I said. "What are going to do with it?"

"It's just a baby cow," he explained. "We are going to fatten it up and eat it. His name is Fred. Would you like to see him?"

He was so enthusiastic I couldn't refuse, so we walked down the dusty road to his house. The Babcock's yard was not very wide, but it was quite deep. Bertie led me to the back corner of the lot and there was Fred. He was encircled by a ring of broken washers, dryers and stoves which formed an inescapable pen. He had no shade and no water. There did not appear to be any entryway into his strange living quarters. Fred looked at me with sad, wet eyes.

Bertie appeared at our kitchen door during my mother's first visit to the farm. I would not let my mother visit us for a few years after our marriage. She had always lived in lovely homes and I knew she would be shocked by our living conditions. When she finally came, the new addition had been added and, although it was not finished, it was certainly more presentable than what I had encountered when I first arrived. She was sitting at the kitchen table, being warmed by the wood stove, when Bertie arrived, smiling as usual. I welcomed him in, although my mother looked at him with a certain degree of repulsion, probably a result of the odor that always seemed to accompany him. I ignored it. As usual, Bertie was smiling and eager to talk. I asked him about school and made small talk. In time, the conversation came to the topic of Fred. I explained to my mother that Fred was a cow the Babcocks were fattening up.

"Oh, Fred," said Bertie. "Well, he died."

"He died?" I asked.

"Yeah," Bertie answered, "but we ate him anyway."

My mother looked down and clasped her hand over her mouth. I was afraid she was going to lose her breakfast. I gently herded Bertie to the door. I wanted my mother to stay longer and I thought she might go upstairs and start packing if Bertie told any more stories.

Bertie had three older sisters. Two were in their teens and evidently fathered by someone other than Robert. Candy had them before she married Robert and, to his credit, he treated them as his own. The next in line was Josie, a skinny waif of a child with freckles on her nose and a crooked-toothed smile. She sometimes came up to Paradise Farm either out of curiosity or jealousy of Bertie. She lacked Bertie's enthusiasm but was good natured and friendly.

"Your house is soooo beautiful!" she used to tell me. "I really like it here."

One day she came looking for Bertie, who had evidently skipped out on his chores.

"I'm sooo tired!" she said, plopping down on a kitchen chair and brushing a lock of brown hair off her forehead. "Our washing machine broke down, so Mom puts the clothes in the bathtub and we take turns stomping on them. Today was my turn and my feet really hurt."

"I'm too little to do that," Bertie said. He turned to Josie and frowned. "We ain't supposed to tell about it. Mom said not to tell."

Josie ignored him. "I stayed up until midnight last night. I watched a program about starving kids in Africa," she said, changing the subject. "I felt so bad I asked my mom if we could do something for them. So we're taking them some stuff we don't need no more."

I was hard put to think of what the Babcocks would have that the Africans would want, but I played along with her.

"How are you going to get it there, Josie?" I asked.

"Mom's going to drive. We got us a station wagon now."

I brought out a globe and showed it to her. "Here is where we live and here is Africa. The blue is water. There are thousands of miles of water between here and Africa. How are you going to get across the ocean?" I asked.

"We'll just go over on the bridge."

I gave up on the geography lesson and brought out the watercolors. Carsten, who had been outside working on the barn, came inside.

"Hi, kids," he said. He then looked at me and said, "Martin's here."

"Martin? I didn't know he was coming. What is he here for?"

"He *is* my son, you know," Carsten snapped. "I guess he wants to see his dad. Also, he has an application form for college and he wants me to help him fill it out."

"And his mother, who has two master's degrees, can't handle it?" I regretted my sarcasm as soon as the words were out of my mouth. I resented the boys coming to the farm only when they wanted or needed something. At least it wasn't money this time.

Carsten glared at me. Martin the Magnificent walked through the kitchen and mumbled "hello" to me. Bertie and Josie continued painting, oblivious to the family tensions.

"Josie told Sarah about about stompin' on the clothes," Bertie said to Carsten without looking up from his art work. "Mom said she wasn't supposed to tell."

Carsten looked puzzled and I mouthed, "I'll tell you later."

Josie glared at Bertie. "I didn't tell her about our sister falling through the bathroom floor," she said.

I had work to do on the addition and left the children in the kitchen. Fifteen minutes later, I went into our office. Carsten was there looking very downcast.

"Where is Martin?" I asked.

"Gone."

"Why did he leave so soon?"

Carsten frowned at me. "He said the children made him too nervous."

"Oh, for God's sake!" I said. "I am so very sorry things here weren't up to Martin the Magnificent's high standards." I stormed from the room before Carsten could respond.

One day Josie and Bertie came to our door laden with new toys. Their dirty faces beamed as they rushed into the house and dumped the toys on the floor.

"My goodness, kids!" I said. "It looks like Christmas! Did Santa get mixed up this year and come in the summer? "

"We got our tax refund!" Josie announced. "We all got new toys and my mom and dad got a waterbed and a stereo."

"And no washing machine," I muttered to myself.

"We just barely got the waterbed into Mom and Dad's room," Bertie said. "They really had trouble with it."

"It must be really big," I said, wondering how the sagging little house could support a waterbed.

"It is so big they had to take the heater in their room out," Josie explained. "Now it fits."

"Do you think the waterbed might freeze in the winter?" I asked.

"Hope not," Bertie said.

Tax refund day was the biggest day of the year at the Babcock's house.

Robert, when not gathering roadkill, training horses or fattening calves, liked to hunt deer, sometimes during hunting season and sometimes not. We did not let him hunt on Paradise Farm. Hunting was one thing Carsten wisely prohibited, because he could imagine Robert shooting wildly at anything, and we always had dogs. He did bag a deer somewhere else and hung the skinned carcass from the swing set in their yard. It was quite dusty that fall and the swing set was near the road. Dust was beginning to coat the carcass.

One day, Robert's parents, clean and well-dressed, were in the side yard, sitting demurely on an old car seat while Robert served them drinks. They were trying to smile while uncomfortably eyeing the deer carcass swaying nearby.

The weather was cold and the snow deep the day I saw the smoke. Carsten and I were avoiding the hazardous roads and working in our office instead of calling on schools. The smoke was black and heavy....it was obviously from a substantial fire not far away. I called for Carsten to look, which he did, but did not show much concern. He then went back to his computer. After watching for a while, I decided to investigate. I walked down the recently plowed road until I could see the Babcock's house. It was totally engulfed in flames. I ran to their neighbor's house. There were Candy and Robert, watching in stunned silence. Tears were rolling down Candy's face. There was a twin hanging on each of her legs.

"Are the other children in school?" I asked.

She didn't speak or look at me. She merely nodded her head. After a few minutes, she gulped back a sob and said, "It's my dogs. They's all in there. I couldn't get them out."

Just then Bill Burns, the local minister, arrived. He told Candy and Robert he was sorry and would try to get them some help from the church.

Robert couldn't take his eyes off of the flaming house. "There goes all my hopes and dreams," he said.

Bill seemed surprised to hear the shack they lived in comprised all of Robert's hopes and dreams. He took a quick look at me, shook his head, and ducked out the door.

At that point, I realized, although Carsten and I didn't have much, we had more than most of the people in Preston. The thought overwhelmed me and I blurted out, "Do you have a place to stay, because we have an empty apartment."

Candy and Robert looked at me with gratitude and Robert said, "Can we stay there? Just until we figure out what to do?"

I said they could and I left the house to walk home through the snow. On the way home, I tried to figure out how I would tell Carsten I had just offered an apartment, which consisted of one large L-shaped room with a sink, a stove and a few cabinets across one wall, one bathroom and one bedroom, to a family of eight. He was more generous than I, but I had no idea how he would accept this arrangement. Even though the care of the apartments often fell upon my shoulders, they really belonged to Carsten. He usually made the big decisions about them.

When I got home, I took a deep breath and told him. I closed my eyes while I waited for his response. He took a long drag on his ever-present pipe and stared at me with those big blue eyes. I was about to apologize and tell him I would retract my invitation when he said, "It's a wonderful thing you just did." I nearly cried tears of relief when he went to get his tools so he could make the needed repairs that always had to be done when we had a new occupant in the apartments. I went with him to the apartment and realized I did not feel the cold. Looking at Carsten made me warm inside.

That evening, the Babcocks moved into the apartment. The move was not difficult, as almost all of their possessions had burned. I was relieved to hear only Candy and the four girls were going to stay there. Robert and the two boys were going elsewhere. For several hours, people arrived bringing clothing, food and even furniture. It was obvious these were people who did not know the Babcocks, but had heard there was a family in need. This was the country version of the Red Cross.

Robert was still around, helping the girls get settled, when Bill Burns arrived with a mattress and a $50 bill. After he left, Robert, who had probably never set foot in the church, complained that they should have given him more than $50.

I noticed Candy's brother, who lived in Preston and was also named Bill, never appeared.

The next day I decided it might be a good idea to set a time limit on the Babcocks' stay in the apartment. I knocked on their door and I was admitted to a room full of mattresses, blankets and assorted bodies. I could get no farther than the doorway.

"Candy," I said, "I think it would be best if we limited your stay to one month at most. I think we should do this so there is no misunderstanding and no hard feelings."

Candy agreed. "You are real nice to do this fer us," she said.

I left feeling good about the arrangement. It was reassuring to know we had a mutual understanding.

A month passed and I told Carsten we had better check to see when the Babcocks were leaving and where they were going. He thought of a creative reason not to go with me and I went to the apartment alone. Candy let me in. The place had not improved from the last time I had been there. It was dirtier and more crowded than it had been a month earlier. I did not see any evidence they were packing.

"Just thought I'd check to see when you were moving out," I said.

Candy was unperturbed. "We ain't found a place yet," she said.

"I told you one month and the month is up," I said, grinning through my teeth.

"And I told you, we ain't found a place yet."

Four little girls' faces glared at me. I walked home, cursing myself for waffling to her. "I'm as big a pushover as Carsten," I mumbled to myself.

Another month passed and they were still there. The weather turned warmer and the children gleefully cut saplings along the road to our house to make teepees in front of the apartments. They kept their horses in their own yard, but periodically rode them around the apartment building, leaving the undeniable evidence behind. Carsten ignored them. My temper, ever present but usually under control, began to erupt. Maxine Marlowe noticed the situation was wearing on me.

"You know, Robert's parents have a nice house in Bradford," she said, "and they were in Florida when the house burned, but they wouldn't let Candy and Robert stay in their house."

My temper boiled a little more, mostly because I realized Robert's parents were smarter than I was.

Maxine was a good source of information about activities in our apartments. She had a good vantage point from her house next door to them.

"A couple of days ago, Candy's new puppy had an accident in the apartment so she shut it up in the car, " Maxine told me. "She left it there for a couple of hours and it tore up the upholstery in her car. It's really a mess!"

"Candy got a puppy?" I exclaimed. I felt myself going over the edge. The addition of a puppy to the mix was more than I could take. All of my self control crumbled and my temper took over. I marched over to the apartment and confronted Candy.

"I understand you have a new puppy," I said as calmly as I could, hoping she wouldn't notice my clenched fists and shaking lips.

"Yep," Candy replied.

"And why, may I ask, did you get a puppy when you are living in our apartment?"

"I just saw him and had to have him," Candy calmly answered, as if her explanation would make me understand.

"That's it, Candy," I said, "you will have to leave. I will give you three days."

They did move out. They moved into a motel in the nearby town of Bradford, because the insurance company was paying the bill. The insurance company paid us three month's rent and we set out to clean up the mess.

The Babcocks came back to Preston from time to time and Robert said to the Marlowes, "Old Carsten was a pretty good guy 'til he married that bitch." The older girls gave me the finger when they saw me. Even Carsten said I was a little harsh with them. Bill, the minister, was the only one who empathized with me.

Eventually, Candy, Robert and family found an old house with a small parcel of land a few miles away. I heard it had no running water. Out of curiosity, I drove past it. It sat up on a small hill and, water or no water, it looked better than their old house. I was happy for Bertie. I even missed him.

I later learned their fire had been caused by creosote in the kitchen wood stove.

THE GOOD, THE BAD AND THE DEERHUNTER

Carsten, while dressed in his business clothes of a suit and tie, once told a man in the next county over that he lived in Preston. The man didn't believe him.

"Why don't you believe me?" Carsten asked.

"Because no one in Preston owns a necktie."

"This is the only one," Carsten said, pointing to his paisley tie. "I lend it out for weddings and funerals."

I never went to any weddings there, but I did go to several funerals. There was not a necktie in sight except for the one around Carsten's neck. The usual Preston attire was blue jeans, worn even at funerals.

In comparison to Preston, Springfield, Illinois, is a metropolis. There, I grew up in an atmosphere of comfort and security. We were not rich, but there was always enough money to provide for us. My older brother, George, my sister, Martha, and I were loved and cared for by our parents and our two adoring, unmarried aunts. Springfield was small enough to be comfortable and large enough to provide some culture.

Because of my father's profession and success as a best-selling author, I was able to meet a few famous people. Adlai Stevenson and Carl Sandberg were two of them. My dad was a favorite of Adlai Stevenson, the governor of Illinois at the time, and he wrote some of Stevenson's non-political speeches. Stevenson called him his "favorite ghost".

I did not spend my early life entirely in Springfield. I went to prep school near Chicago and to college in the East. I was more familiar with large cities than small towns. I planned to move to Chicago after college, but my father's death caused me to change my plans.

When I moved to Preston, I had preconceived notions about small towns. I did not expect to meet famous people or to find much culture. Friendliness is the attribute most often associated with small towns, yet, after I had been there for two months, no one had spoken to me. I went to the post office and the grocery store, but no one's curiosity was piqued. I thought a new face in town would be noticed but, evidently, my presence was not worth comment. This was puzzling and I wondered aloud to Carsten about it.

"They don't ask you anything, because they already know all about you," he said.

Shortly after my arrival, I was involved in an automobile accident in which I broke the windshield with my head. I was not seriously injured, but I was required to wear a large collar to restrict movement of my head and neck. While wearing it, I went to the general store. There, talking to Gary, was one of my favorite characters in Preston. I called him The Deerhunter. I had seen him many times before, dressed in camouflage. That day was no different. As usual, he was ready, just in case he saw a huge buck.

He was about 75 years old and had white hair and eyes of cobalt blue that twinkled when he smiled. The most amazing thing about him was his beard. He always had about a one-half inch or five-day growth of white stubble. I never could figure out how he did that. His last name was Rockwinder, so everyone called him Rocky. I never did learn his real first name. He had never spoken to me before, but on that day he looked at me and then at Gary.

"Her old man got so mad at her he broke her neck," he said to Gary.

Highly excited, I left the store and hurried home. "Carsten!" I shouted as I walked in the door. "Rocky, the deerhunter, spoke to me today! He's the first person in town to do that."

"What did he say?"

"Well, he didn't actually speak to me, but he acknowledged my presence."

"That's a start," Carsten said. "Before you know it you'll be invited to join the quilting club."

That simple act of recognition endeared Rocky to me. He was considered a ne'er-do-well by the townsfolk because, when there was a choice between fishing, hunting or working on his poor little farm, he never chose farming. He loved to fish in our pond. He was usually accompanied by two other men, who were about his same age. They were the unelected elders of the town. One was called Red, even though his hair had long ago turned white. He was a retired truck driver and the teamsters gave him a good enough pension to have a comfortable life. He was the best known man in town and, if the place had been incorporated, he probably would have been the mayor. Red usually had a complaint about something that was happening in Preston. More often than not, he was half mad at Rocky. "That goldurned Rocky," he would mutter. "Fishes with a string, a stick and a safety pin, then he catches the biggest fish in the pond. Makes no sense. B'God, he oughter be farmin', but he'll find any excuse not to work."

Red loved to fish and hunt for morel "mush-er-rooms" (put the accent on the last syllable). He introduced me to mushroom hunting, an activity I still have a passion for. Although he was approaching 80 and could hardly bend over, he had a real knack for finding morels and mushrooms he called Andy Gumps. He would point with his walking stick or gently push a leaf aside and spot those elusive morels I would never have seen. Because bending down was no longer an option for him, I had the thrill of picking them. Carsten decided we couldn't possibly know what we were doing and the "mush-er-rooms" were most likely poison. Therefore, after dividing them up with Red, I got to eat all of mine.

Red and his wife of over fifty years had raised and educated four children who had all moved out of town, except for the youngest boy, Johnny, who had Down's Syndrome. Johnny was in his twenties and attended a special school. When at home, he was expected to do simple chores and join in family activites. He was given wonderful care.

Red's wife was a steadfast member of the Preston Methodist Church and Red was just as steadfast in his refusal to set foot in the church. "B'God, I'm just as good a man as that cheatin' son 'a bitch preacher from the church in Farleyville that lives next door to me," he would proclaim, in defense of his antipathy for religion. His wife quietly held on to her religious beliefs without trying to change Red's.

The third town elder was Hans, who ran a barber shop in nearby Bradford. He had a sweetness about him the others lacked. He was never critical, but loved to fish and swap stories with his friends. He and his lovely wife lived in a neat-as-a-pin house and unassumingly gave a little class to the town.

One afternoon in the early spring, Rocky worked on his farm. It must not have been a good day for fishing. When it was time for his supper, he sat down on the edge of a wagon to remove his muddy shoes. He got one shoe off, but died before he could remove the second one. Several days later, as I watched his casket being lowered into a grave in the town cemetery, I thought, Rocky never should have worked that day.

Near the center of town lived a good-for-nothing named Bill Dempsey. Because the minister of the Preston Methodist Church was also named Bill, Carsten and I distinguished between them by calling them Good Bill and Bad Bill.

Bad Bill's frame house was completely devoid of paint. The windows were so dirty curtains or shades would have been redundant. The only green thing in his yard was the scum on the water sitting stagnant in his front yard.

He was on his third or fourth wife and he had sired children by all of them. The latest wife had three children by him and they were often seen playing in the stagnant water. I became suspicious when the puddle did not diminish during a summer drought. Then I realized it wasn't the rain from above creating the puddle, but the septic tank from below.

An old electric fan on a tall stand and a rusted-out gas stove also sat in his yard. A sign remained there for several years advertising a garage sale.

I don't know what, if anything, Bad Bill did for a living. He spent most of his time in court for neglecting to pay child support. He was Candy Babcock's brother. Like Candy, Bad Bill knew how to live off the land. He carried a shotgun with him most of the time and shot at anything that moved, including several local dogs. I still think he killed our dog Beau-Beau, but I could never prove it.

One evening, while Carsten and I were in our yard, we heard a gunshot followed by shotgun pellets peppering the tree tops over our heads. The shot came from the direction of the railroad track that formed the southern border of our farm, so we walked down there and found Bad Bill with one of his sons.

"What are you doing?" we asked.

Bad Bill looked perturbed. "Hunting," he replied.

"You just shot into our property and right over our heads," Carsten said, while doing an admirable job of controlling his temper. "So what, exactly, are you hunting for?"

"I like to walk the tracks and shoot small game. Then I leave it to attract larger game," Bad Bill explained.

"Oh, like lions and tigers?" I said, sarcastically.

Carsten took my arm and led me away. His motive was either to avoid a confrontation or to keep me safe from this man. In any event, it was probably the wisest thing to do at the time. We notified the sheriff's office and told the deputy Bad Bill shot across a fence row into our yard, which is illegal.

"It is?" the deputy said.

We decided not to pursue the matter further. Law enforcement in the area was very loose and it was probably best not to tangle with Bad Bill.

One night, Good Bill went out to his garage behind the church and found a large hog had wandered into it and did not seem inclined to leave. He was contemplating what to do when Bad Bill arrived in a state of high animation. He had seen the hog and was salivating over the prospect of pork chops.

"Wow!'" he exclaimed. "How about that? What say we split him?"

Good Bill didn't understand. He asked for an explanation.

"Split him!" yelled Bad Bill. "I've got a sword and I can do it right here in your garage."

Good Bill groped for an excuse. "I don't want the mess in my garage," he said.

"We can take it out in the back yard," Bad Bill said.

"Someone might see us there, and it wouldn't look good for the minister to be killing someone else's hog," Good Bill said.

Bad Bill realized that his dream of free pork was not going to come to fruition and skulked off into the night.

I was in the general store one day when Bad Bill entered.

"Know where I can get videos?" he asked Gary.

"Videos?" Gary asked back.

"Yep. Movies on tape. Just got myself a video cassette recorder and I wanna rent me some videos."

VCR players had only recently become available. I knew only a few people who owned one. It would be several years before Gary began renting videos. I waited until Bad Bill left the store to approach Gary.

"Well, I'm so glad he has a VCR, aren't you?"

"Yeh," Gary said, shaking his head. "His kids come in here barefoot with ragged clothes and filthy faces and here he is buying a VCR. What a creep."

"Did you ever hear about the man in a small town who terrorized the townsfolk so much they were afraid to go outside when he was around?" I asked.

"No."

"Well, they got tired of him so they all got together and planned how to get rid of him. They lured him into town and about ten or fifteen of them shot him simultaneously in broad daylight. When the law came, not a single person would claim to be a witness."

"When you shoot Bill, I won't tell," said Gary.

"Same for me, Gary. I won't breathe a word if you do it."

In competition with Bad Bill for the worst scum in town was the son of the local beauty operator. He had been in jail many times for attempted rape. He was once caught hiding in the church organist's garage and another time trying to break into a home in a neighboring town to get at the minister's wife. He apparently had an attraction to the ladies of the church. Luckily, he was not successful at anything he did, so he never accomplished the terrible deed. Everyone breathed easier when he was back in jail, where he spent most of his time.

Next to the church was a ramshackle house full of a large family named Mosley. They did one thing well, and that was reproduce. Mrs. Mosley never spoke to me, but I would see her around town with her head hung low to avoid looking at or speaking to anyone. She had a husband, but he was not often in evidence. One of their sons, whose name was Dillon, rode the bus to high school with my son, Dan. Dillon was putting in his required hours at school, just waiting to drop out so he could spend his time doing more productive things like drinking and partying. He once asked Carsten if he could have a little campout with his friends down at our pond. Carsten did not know how to refuse anyone anything, so he allowed it. After three days, Dillon and friends were still there. There were girls and beer and I'm sure there were some new Mosleys made down there. Carsten finally went down to the pond and told them they had to leave. The next day the tires on our plow were slashed.

I saw a three-year-old girl in the store one day and asked Gary who she belonged to.

"She's one of the Mosleys," he said.

"I didn't know they had any children that young," I replied. "I thought Dillon was one of the youngest."

Gary hesitated. He was clearly having trouble deciding what to tell me. I waited patiently.

"She's really not one of the children," he said. "They're raising her like she is, but she's the daughter's kid. She had her when she was a sophomore in high school."

A young man in his twenties named Ivan Morton lived in a tiny house behind a modest Preston residence. He had the mentality of a ten year old. We called him Drivin' Ivan because he was often seen zooming around town on his moped, which had a large American flag decal on the windshield. If there was ever a good place for someone like Ivan, this was it. No stigma was attached to his condition and, because the locals looked out for his welfare, he was able to live alone and have a productive life. Dirty Del gave him errands to run and odd jobs to do around his garage. Ivan took his responsibilities very seriously and had a look of determination on his face when performing his duties.

One day, Ivan came up to the farm with a message from Dirty Del. Carsten's legs were sticking out from under the house and I was handing tools to him as he fixed a leaky pipe.

"Hi, Ivan," I said. "We have a problem here."

Ivan's demeanor changed from a smile to a look of real concern and empathy. When he spoke, his voice rose from deep in his throat.

"Unh, unh," he grunted. "I HATE problems."

That little expression struck us as so appropriate that we used it constantly. We had many problems, and we, too, hated them.

෴

The big birthday for many of the Preston teens was sixteen, because then they could drop out of school. Those who did nearly always married young and had children young.....a sure prescription for a lifetime of poverty.

When we heard of a couple getting a divorce, we usually heard a few days later that one of them was getting married again. The new spouse was often someone who lived within a one-mile radius of Preston. The horizons there were very small.

"Don't ever talk about anybody here," Carsten warned me. "They're all related to each other, either by blood or marriage. It's very consanguine."

Carsten once saw graffiti in a public bathroom that said, in typical Hoosier spelling, "Insest is best. A sport the whole family can enjoy." Evidently that "sport" occurred in the area of Preston. Rocky once told me there was a boy in the area who was the product of incest.

"How do you know?" I asked.

"You'll know when you see him," he responded.

Ironically, it was at Rocky's funeral that I saw this boy. I knew him when I saw him. His bald pate was interrupted only occasionally by tufts of colorless hair. His skin was yellowish-brown. His eyes were slits and his eyelids had no visible lashes. I never saw him again.

There came a time when I felt I could no longer be both wife and business partner to Carsten. Living in isolation like we did left no breathing room from each other and I tendered my resignation from the business.

For a long time, I had watched the children of Preston heading for nowhere and felt I could help them. With the cooperation of the Methodist minister, I formulated a plan. Armed with many old Apple IIe computers and floppy discs we used to sell, I set up a free tutoring service two nights a week. The computers and software were technologically outdated but educationally sound. A woman parishioner from the church helped me and we taught reading, writing and math to several of the local elementary and middle school children. The elementary school teachers told me our students' reading skills improved greatly.

One of the middle school students was the son of our neighbor, who was a mechanic and who owned snow plowing equipment. After I tutored his son, he always made sure our driveway was plowed when it snowed.

Bradley was our most special student. He was a disheveled kid of about ten, who had one foot that turned in, making his walk ungainly. He had sandy hair and freckles and lived in a trailer with his parents and two younger siblings. His father was a Viet Nam vet with post traumatic stress disorder, and his mother was a large woman who looked as if she had given up on life. Both parents were heavy smokers and full to overflowing ashtrays sat on the kitchen table and counters. The air inside was barely breathable. Going into their place was always a depressing experience.

Brad was a quiet kid who attended tutoring regularly and made good progress. One evening, he arrived looking particularly dirty and beaten down. I took both of his hands in mine and looked him in the eye.

"Brad," I said, "look at you. Your hair is dirty and uncombed. Your shirt is buttoned wrong and your shirttail is hanging out on one side. Your shoes are dirty and untied. Brad, you are somebody. You are as important as anyone else. I want you to look at yourself in the mirror and say, 'I am Brad Griffith. I am going to show the world that I can be clean and handsome and smart. I am worth something and I am worth taking care of.'"

Brad looked at me in his quiet way and hung his head. I had no idea how he would react to my speech.

The next time he came to tutoring class, his hair was wet and smelled of shampoo. His clothes were clean and neat and his shoes were tied. Later that week, his teacher called me and said that he was now reading almost up to grade level. I considered my experience with Brad to be one of the most rewarding of my time in Preston.

BRADFORD..... CLOSE TO THE EDGE

The closest real town to Preston was Bradford, which had a population of 5,000 or 7,000, depending on which atlas you believed. It was hard not to like the place. The old buildings downtown had been retained, because no one could afford to tear them down. They were Bradford's biggest asset. Most of them were kept in good repair and had a certain quaintness and charm. They were painted with a palette of colors suggested by the wife of Preston's postmaster.

A train track bisected the town and the graffiti on the viaduct read "Welcomb Home" and "Marry Christmas." Compared to Chicago graffiti, that was downright refreshing.

The local paper's classified ads once advertised a bouffee for sale, which had me stumped until I realized it was listed under used furniture and I sounded it out. Buffet !

The residents poked fun at themselves by wearing sweatshirts that said:

"Bradford, Indiana.....
It's not the end of the world
But you can see it from there"

Bradford's claim to fame, while I lived in Indiana, was the state championship trophy won by its high school basketball team. Indiana loves basketball and, during the 80's, the small schools competed with the large ones. The championship put the town in a state of euphoria for several years.

A small river wound through town and flooded about every fourth year. The residents said they would rather live on the river than anywhere else in town, so they cheerfully shoveled the muck out of their living rooms and basements and enjoyed a dry house for a few years, only to have it happen all over again.

When I told other Hoosiers I lived near Bradford, I would receive puzzling responses.

"Do you ever go outside when the wind is blowing from Bradford toward your house?"

"Have they fixed their problem yet?"

"I always know when I'm passing Bradford."

I assumed they were referring to the floods, so I never mentioned the comments to Carsten or asked him about them.

One day, when I was at the drive-through window of the bank, a terrible odor wafted through my car. I was sure I had run over an animal and its dead and decaying body was suspended from the undercarriage. I jumped out of the car and started looking all around and underneath it. The lady in the car behind me looked at me as if I were crazy, or, as the local residents would say, "mental".

"I don't know what that awful smell is," I explained.

Her response was unexpected. She began to laugh. She didn't seem to notice there was a strange and terrible odor in the air.

When I returned home, I related the incident to Carsten. He, too, began to laugh.

"That's the fertilizer plant. Haven't you smelled it before?"

"No," I said. "What kind of fertilizer do they make? I've never smelled anything quite so putrid."

"They make fertilizer out of dead animals," Carsten explained. "The plant is on the east side of town and when the wind is blowing out of the east, it really stinks up the area. Bradford is famous for it. Sometimes I can smell it out here, even though we're eight miles away."

I soon came to realize there was a dark side to Bradford. I noticed the complete absence of people of color and minorities in the town. When I remarked on this to Carsten's secretary, a Bradford resident, she said, "Oh, they come sometimes, but they're encouraged to leave real fast." There were also no Jews, or at least there was no synagogue. The town was completely homogeneous. White Christians were the only ones "welcomb" there.

All of the utility companies servicing Preston were located in Bradford, including the telephone company. It was the first of the service industries I had to deal with, because I called to request a new phone line. They told me I would have to have an eight-party line, as there were no more private lines available.

"Eight parties! I've never heard of an eight-party line!" I exclaimed. "How can I conduct business on an eight-party line?"

The telephone company stood its ground. "Lady, that's all we have right now. It's either that or no phone at all."

An irate Carsten called them and spiced up his complaint with a few choice words and some legal threats. Shortly afterwards, I miraculously received a private line. I found the incident so unusual I told Carsten's secretary about it.

"The phone company is very weird," she said. "A friend of mine has a small business in her house and she requested a separate phone line for the business. The phone company obliged and sent a serviceman. When he was finished, he asked her if she wanted a bell. She asked what he meant and he said he wanted to know if she wanted a ringer on her phone. She said of course she did and wondered why anyone wouldn't want a bell. 'Some people only want to call out,' he said."

"Oh, yeah," I said, after I had finished laughing. "Why would anyone want to be bothered by a ringing phone at their business?"

Our educational materials business required us to spend much of our time on the phone. Unfortunately, we had continuing problems with the phone company. When it rained, there was so much static on the line we couldn't hear. One day Carsten called them and complained he could barely hear people on the other end of the line. It was not raining, so static was not a problem, but the voices were very faint.

"Where are you located?" the telephone lady asked.

"Preston."

"Maybe you can't hear because you're so far away," she explained.

Carsten couldn't contain his anger. "I talk to people in California every day! That's two thousand miles away! Bradford is eight miles away! I hardly think that's the problem!"

He slammed down the receiver.

"I guess she thinks we talk through a tube," he said.

Bradford had its idiosyncrasies and the phone company was not alone in its strange business practices. The retail stores had a habit of arguing with customers when they had a complaint.

One particular incident illustrates their attitude. Carsten had worn glasses for most of his life and he needed stronger lenses. Prescription in hand, he went to the oculist in Bradford and ordered a new pair of glasses. When he got them, he realized the frames did not fit properly. He took them back to the store and told them he would have to have different frames.

"What's the matter with these?" the sullen girl at the desk inquired.

"When I smile, my cheeks push the glasses up and they also get smudged from touching my face."

She had an easy solution. "Don't smile," she said.

Carsten's eyes were a problem. He could do nothing without his glasses. Then, his eyes began giving him more trouble than usual. He complained that they seemed irritated. After a week of watching him rub his eyes, I insisted he go to the ophthalmologist. He finally made an appointment. I drove him there in case they dilated his pupils and he couldn't drive home. When I went to pick him up, he had a strange look on his face.

"Well," I said, "what did the doctor say?"

"He was very puzzled," Carsten said. "He looked in my eyes. Then he looked again. Then he got out a huge medical book and started looking things up in there."

I was getting worried. What if he had a rare and incurable eye condition? "Go on," I urged.

"He said I have follicles on my eyeballs."

I hesitated. "Carsten, I only know about one kind of follicle and that is a hair follicle."

"That's what I have," he said.

I couldn't wait to tell Amy. We had often teased Carsten about being very hairy and he even referred to himself as hirsute.

"Hairy eyeballs!" she exclaimed when I told her. "Well, Carsten you are never going to live this one down."

A few years after I moved there, a new business appeared between Bradford and Preston. It was a vacation park for campers. The developers bought a large field and immediately cut down huge oak trees, many of which were more than 100 years old. They flattened out all of the undulations in the earth, dug a little pond and put in asphalt roads. They built a club house, a swimming pool and a tennis court.

Soon the campers began to arrive. They bought tiny tracts of land just large enough for their trailers and parked them there permanently. They put up little awnings and strung Japanese lanterns on them. These would be their vacation homes.

The employees of the park wore pink, aqua or pale green jumpsuits. They rode around in golf carts as did the campers.

The park was not aesthetically appealing and I felt it was something of a scar on the landscape. The local residents did not agree. The park was voted "Best Business of the Year" by the Bradford Chamber of Commerce.

Bradford had several nice stores, but very few good places to eat. It had a "bouffee" that specialized in steak. Pictures of the champion cattle they had purchased….and we were about to eat…..

were displayed on the wall. While waiting in line, the customers were expected to admire these steaks on the hoof. After about two visits there, one of which involved a malfunctioning machine that nearly engulfed Carsten with soft serve ice cream, we decided to eat elsewhere. We discovered a Chinese restaurant with decent food and we usually ate there when we were in town. It was owned by a beautiful and gracious Chinese woman and I suspected Carsten was more attracted to her than to the food she served.

One evening we went to the restaurant and the lady wasn't there. Instead, we were greeted by a Chinese couple. He was in his early 40s, small and thin with large, black-rimmed glasses. She was about twenty years old and absolutely beautiful. They smiled and nodded to us while leading us to a booth.

"Where is the lady who was here before?" we asked.

They smiled and nodded.

"Did you buy this place?" we asked.

They smiled and nodded.

"Yes, yes," he said, as he handed us menus.

A couple at the next booth motioned to us. "They're the new owners," they whispered. "They only know a few words of English."

Carsten didn't seem disappointed and I noticed him looking at the new young female owner with approval. I couldn't blame him; she was lovely. When she came to take our orders, instead of speaking, we pointed to the items we wanted on the menu.

The food was excellent and, even though we did not eat out often, when we did, it was usually there. Because they did not have many customers, they would come and talk to us. Her name was Ling and he was Chin. Conversation was difficult, but they were learning English. Ling was taking classes in English and was progressing faster than Chin.

Chin was bewildered by the lack of customers. There was another Chinese restaurant in town that had more success, even though their food was not nearly as good. The difference was the other restaurant had a liquor license and they did not.

"Why they not come here?" he complained to us one evening. "Lady we buy this place from say business good.'"

We were reluctant to tell him he needed to sell liquor. We did not know why they didn't have a liquor license and were hesitant to bring up what might have been a delicate subject.

As we pondered what to say, Chin said, "Maybe it the lock-shun."

Carsten and I looked at each other. We could usually make some sense out of his English, but this one had us baffled.

"The lock-shun! The lock-shun!" he repeated.

Still we sat, looking at him blankly. He ran to get his Chinese-English dictionary and was frantically flipping through the pages when it came to me.

"Location!" I exclaimed. "That's it, location!"

"Yes, yes," he said, smiling. "That it. Lock-shun. Telephone company right down street. But they no come here. Walk right by at lunch time. One day I sweep sidewalk. Man walk by and say 'Fah goo.' I just sweep sidewalk. Why he say 'fah goo' to me?"

Carsten looked confused. This was one I could understand and I kicked him under the table. I mouthed "F U" and he finally got it. Once again, we could not answer Chin's question.

The couple quickly had two baby boys and worked very hard to make the restaurant succeed, but their business did not improve. The struggle began to show in Chin's appearance. He seemed to be deteriorating. His black-rimmed glasses were now held together at the nose piece with white adhesive tape. He was clean shaven except for three long black hairs protruding from his Adam's apple. Ling looked exhausted. She was doing a lion's share of the work. She only became animated when she told us about her attempts to bring her twin sisters to the U.S. Carsten couldn't wait. The thought of two more beautiful women like Ling in Bradford was certainly something he was looking forward to. I, too, was anxious for their arrival, because I was sure, if they came to Bradford and worked in the restaurant, we would be eating out a lot more often. Her request was denied, however, and they never came. After that, Ling seemed to lose the small amount of vivacity she had left.

One night I told Carsten I was tired of cooking and really needed a night out. He reluctantly consented to take me to Bradford for dinner, even though he would have rather stayed home. As usual, we went to the Chinese restaurant. It was closed. A passerby said Chin and Ling had moved away to a larger city in Indiana. We were very sorry we had not had a chance to tell them goodbye. Because we were in the mood for Chinese food, we went to the other Chinese restaurant. It, too, was closed.

"What is going on here?" I asked Carsten.

He was as bewildered as I. "I guess the Asian invasion has ended," he said. "Bradford just isn't ready for non-white, non-Christian people." Then he smiled his "I got my way this time" smile. "It looks like you'll have to cook dinner tonight after all."

"Fah-goo," I said.

The next day, the paper detailed the demise of the second Chinese restaurant. The health inspectors had gone there and had found it to be extremely dirty. However, the discovery of dogs in the basement was what had prompted an immediate shutdown. Carsten and I had just missed being served Egg Foo Fido.

WHAT TERRIBLE SIN
DID YOU COMMIT?

On our doorstep stood a tall, clean-cut young man. He wore horn-rimmed glasses, khaki pants, and a blue, button-down oxford shirt. His hair was clean and close-cropped. He was obviously an alien. A towheaded little girl of about six was with him.

I gave an unenthusiastic greeting. Uninvited guests in Preston could be unwelcome surprises. I waited for this person to explain who he was.

"My name is Bill Burns. I am the new minister of the Preston Methodist Church."

I couldn't speak. How could this be? I had seen the previous minister around town and he seemed to fit right in with the community. He was short and rotund, and had a penchant for yellow polyester suits and bird watching.

Here on our doorstep stood his replacement.

My disbelief took my breath away. I stared at Bill's outstretched hand and finally, realizing my manners had taken a leave of absence, I grasped it and was able to blurt out, "And where do you come from, Mr. Bill?"

"Well, I grew up in Ohio, and I recently graduated from Yale Divinity School."

That did it. I needed help here.

"Carsten!" I called. "Come here, quick!"

Mr. Bill stood on the porch. By the look on his face, I could tell he thought I was crazy.

When Carsten appeared, I did the introductions. "This is Bill," I gasped. "He is the new minister at the Methodist church and he is a graduate of Yale."

Carsten started to jump. Just little hops like he did when something was so funny he was temporarily without words. This, I might add, was an unusual condition for my husband. When he regained his composure, he asked, "What terrible sin did you commit that they sent you here?"

Bill's glad-to-meet-you smile vanished. As a newcomer, he couldn't understand what Carsten meant, but I knew he would in time.

The little girl at his side, who was tagging along with him, lived with her mother in one of our apartments. In spite of the fact that we had just arrived home from a trip and were surrounded by luggage and boxes, we invited them both in. As we chatted with Bill, whom we found to be a delightful young man, the little girl kept walking around our piano. She asked me to play it and I told her I didn't play very well and only played when no one was listening. She continued to investigate the piano, looking around the sides, back and front. Finally, she put her hands on her hips and, in an exasperated voice, said, "How do you turn this thing on, anyway?"

I looked at Bill and smiled. I really wanted to say, "Fella, you ain't heard nuthin' yet!"

In time, Bill became a friend of ours. To distinguish him from the town creep, Bill Dempsey, we dubbed the minister "Good Bill". He often stopped by for conversation with Carsten. Carsten, though raised a Catholic, was not a religious man and would never consider entering a church. He was, however, a philosophy major, and could talk about ideas spiritual and intellectual with Bill. We sometimes invited him to dine with us and I enjoyed sitting and talking at the kitchen table with him. He was usually discreet about discussing the parishioners, but occasionally he had trouble hiding his feelings.

"You know that couple that lives in the little house next to the cemetery?" Bill asked.

"I only know who they are," I said. "We have never spoken."

"She keeps to herself and doesn't socialize with anyone," Bill said.

"She sure has a beautiful garden," I said. "Carsten almost went off the road because he was looking at the garden. At least that's what he said. I'm sure he wasn't looking at her!"

Bill laughed. The woman loved to work in the garden in very short shorts and tiny skintight tops. She was blond and beautiful and was admired from afar by many Preston men.

"You know, her husband is Jewish," Bill said.

"No, I didn't know that. He has to be Preston's first Jew."

"Some ladies from the church came to me and asked me to try to convert him."

I shook my head. "She doesn't go to church, does she?"

"No."

"And they want you to convert him to Christianity?"

"Yes."

"Ah, God bless Hoosier homogeneity!" I said.

Good Bill had arrived in our community an enthusiastic and idealistic reformer. He had not been sent to us because he committed a terrible sin, as Carsten had implied. He had asked the church to place him in a poor rural community. He would put his idealism to the test here.

The local Methodists provided its ministers with a substantial red brick house directly behind the church. It stood in sharp contrast to the decaying, paintless houses of Bad Bill Dempsey on one side and the Mosleys on the other. Bill tried to minister to the downtrodden of the area and didn't have to look far to do this. One of his self-appointed missions was to help parolees get back on their feet.

A strange new face soon appeared in town and I learned it belonged to one of Bill's "projects." The man was a thief who was out on parole. Bill had visited him in prison and offered to help him adjust to the outside. He went so far as to take him into his house.

The parolee wasn't there long. One night, he paired up with his brother-in-law and set out to rob a drug store in the small vil-

lage a few miles to the north. This wasn't to be a minor misde-
meanor. They had guns. They waited until dark and staked out the
store. The brother-in-law proceeded down the road to the store
while Bill's parolee friend stood lookout. What happened next is
unclear, but the parolee somehow shot himself in the foot and the
caper was over before it started.

"Can you believe that?" Bill asked us. "He was so dumb they
hadn't even robbed anything yet and he goes and shoots himself in
the foot! Of course, they put him in jail again, because he violated
his parole just by having a gun."

"Disenchantment number one," I thought to myself. Bill was
already showing signs of losing his altruism and magnanimity.

Good Bill stayed for a few years. His enthusiasm diminished a
little each year and he was eventually transferred to a much larger
community. Before he left, he said to me, "You know, after living
here, I have come to believe some people deserve to be poor."

Bill Burns was succeeded by a lovely woman minister named
Denise. She was young, pretty, smart and ambitious. She was working on her doctoral degree and took the job with the small church
because it was fairly close to her university and did not require as
much time as a large congregation would. She met with Bill several
times after she began her tenure there. Even though their meetings were church-related and not intended to be romantic, she fell
in love with him.

Denise, like Bill, visited us often to use our computer or just to
visit. She and Carsten had many long talks. It was Carsten she told
of her love for Bill. Bill, however, had met someone else through
his new job and he soon married her. Denise was disappointed but
was very busy with her school and the church. She mentioned Bill
occasionally and hurt flickered momentarily in her eyes, but she
moved on.

Denise stayed for a few years until she finished her doctorate.
We grew as fond of her as we had of Bill. She did wonderful things
for the church, even though her schedule at school was demanding.

"You had better be careful," I would say to her. "You are doing such a good job here, they won't let you leave!"

She laughed at this. Her ambitions reached far beyond a tiny community like Preston.

I felt a certain kinship with Denise. I enjoyed having a woman to talk to and she helped me set up the tutoring program at the church.

When I told her about my experiences in Springfield with Luke Churchill and his promiscuity, she said, "Presbyterians are known for that!"

Denise owned a cat when she arrived in Preston and soon acquired a dog. At around 3 a.m. one morning, her dog started growling and her cat's hair stood on end. They both stared at the front door. Denise got out of bed and stood in the front hall. The handle of the front door was moving. She made sure the lock was secure and then went to call the sheriff.

"Someone is trying to break into my house!" she told the deputy. She described the scene.

"Call me back and tell me what happens," the officer replied.

Denise insisted they send someone to her house, which they reluctantly did. When they arrived, they found the town rapist in a field not far from the manse with a lock-picking tool in his pocket. He was taken into custody, but his friend, Dillon Mosley, who had sliced our plow's tires in appreciation for letting him use our pond, bailed him out in a few hours.

The town rapist, who was the son of the local beautician, seemed to always go after church people. Once again he failed in his attempts....with no thanks to the local sheriff's department.

Denise's dog was shot with a shotgun a few months later by persons unknown. The dog survived, but had hundreds of pellets in him.

Denise was not the same after those two incidents. She was nervous and unable to completely relax again. She finished her doctorate and moved to Chicago.

The people of Preston took her departure in stride. They gave her a going away party like they had done for so many who had gone before her. Then they waited for the Methodist Church to send them the next one.

A few years into our marriage, we hired a cleaning lady. She was a large woman named Daisy, whom I found through a newspaper ad. She stated in the ad she was a Christian.

She was pleasant and a good worker who had intelligence and artistic talents. I wondered why she was cleaning houses for a living.

She belonged to a large fundamentalist church and spoke of it often. It was a very important part of her life. The church was 25 miles north of us in the city of South Bend and was owned and ministered to by a man named Doctor Lester Sumrall.

"Any other church seems like kindergarten after you've heard Dr. Sumrall," Daisy said.

Doctor Lester Sumrall built a dynasty with a television station, a large church, a K-12 school and a college. I heard of his accomplishments long before I ever saw him or met Daisy.

Soon my curiosity overcame my distrust of religious leaders and I watched him on television. There he was, a balding, homely man, with no detectable charisma. He was delivering his New Year's message. With misplaced modifiers, sentence-ending prepositions, and lack of subject-verb agreement, he proclaimed he received his message straight from God. I began to wonder why he had such a large following and how he obtained his doctorate without a rudimentary knowledge of the English language. Then I thought about his enterprises: he had his own television station and he founded his own schools from elementary all the way through college. I suspected his degree was self-bestowed.

Because of my church experiences in Illinois, I was no longer a churchgoer, so I was free on Sunday mornings to watch Dr. Sumrall's question and answer show. I watched in amazement as Lester presided over an adoring and trusting congregation. People sent in questions which were read to Lester by one of his sons. The son assured the congregation Lester had not seen the questions before and he received the answers straight from God. When Lester's son filled in for him some Sunday mornings, he was always careful to say God did not speak directly to him. Only Lester received His true message. One of the questions was as follows:

"Dr. Sumrall, I am a farmer and a Christian. My neighbor is a farmer and not a Christian. Every year he has a better crop than I do. Why?"

I was sure I knew the answer. Maybe his neighbor was a better farmer. Maybe his soil was richer. Maybe he worked harder. That's what I thought God would say. But, no. I was wrong. God told Lester to say, "Well, how good a Christian are you? Do you tithe?"

Lester also liked to tell stories about his religious feats….. especially the exorcisms he performed. He was quite impressed with money and usually prefaced his stories with "A very rich family…….." He contended God wants Christians to be rich, and he seemed to equate wealth with Godliness. His television station aired many programs about making money.

One of Lester's stories concerned "a very rich family" living in California. While he was visiting them, they invited him to spend the night. He readily accepted because they had a very nice house, but there was one problem: he would have to sleep in the spare bedroom….. and it was haunted. Lester was not deterred. Everything went fine until about 3 a.m., when a lady ghost appeared in the closet. Lester told her to go away, but she wouldn't. She seemed to be looking for a dead baby. Lester attempted several times to make her go away, but she still refused. So, of course, as any person would, he started tearing up the floor boards in the closet. The next morning, his hosts were quite dumbfounded that he had done this. He told them he had exorcised the ghost and they need not worry about her anymore. I think they had new worries with their floor all torn up, but I guess it was a fair trade.

From that house he went to another house of yet another rich family. They had real problems. Their son was possessed—not by the devil, but by a spirit they were reluctant to discuss. They evidently had heard of Lester's powers and turned to him in desperation.

Lester arrived at their large, beautiful home and met the distraught parents. Suddenly, their son came running down the stairs. He was screaming, "I am the spirit of masturbation! I am the spirit of masturbation!" Lester was not intimidated. He met that spirit head on and exorcised it. He never explained exactly how he did it, but I wish he had. It would have made a really good story.... and provided a useful solution to a widespread problem.

I often saw Daisy on television when I watched Lester's Sunday morning show; she nodded and smiled along with everyone else as she listened to Lester's words of wisdom. She, along with the rest of the congregation, had complete faith in Lester. They believed in his powerful connection to God and in his ability to take care of them. Daisy had no health insurance and didn't feel she needed it. She was sure Lester or God could heal her if she got sick.

When Amy had two wisdom teeth pulled, her face blew up like a balloon. Daisy, who happened to be cleaning our house that day, took one look at her and asked if she could try to heal her. What did we have to lose? She laid her hands on Amy's face and closed her eyes. Looking to the heavens, she spoke in tongues.

"Ah boo kah bah troy plo mahlah," Daisy chanted.

Amy's eyes were as big as saucers, but I motioned to her to lie still. Daisy finished and stood back to watch the miracle. Nothing happened. She was stunned. "I thought she would be healed," she said, dejectedly. "I guess only Lester has the powers."

LESSER LESSORS

After graduating from college, I returned home to live with my mother. I got a job teaching first grade at a school in a poor section of town. Some of the children lived outside of the city in an area facetiously called Hollywood. They were squatters of a sort and their houses were not regulated by any building codes. Some of the people built their own houses with materials salvaged from the junk yard. Many had no plumbing. I came home in the evenings with tales of neglect, abuse and just plain poverty.

My mother would listen in disgust. She would cross her long, thin legs, light a cigarette and blow out smoke in a loud puff. (She never inhaled.)

"Oh, those people!" she would say. "They ought to be sterilized!"

The apartments on our property reminded me of my mother.

When Carsten bought the farm, it included the farm house, 30 tillable acres of farm land, an old orchard, woods and an apartment building. The previous owner thought it would be a good investment to build a perfectly square building, divide it into equal parts and create four efficiency apartments on an untillable parcel of land that was close to the town, but still a part of the farm.

The building was constructed with the cheapest materials available. The four units were identical, each having an L-shaped living room/dining room/kitchen combination, one bedroom in which was the only closet, and a bathroom. The kitchen consisted of a few cabinets, a sink, a stove and a refrigerator along one wall. The floors were carpeted with green indoor/outdoor carpeting glued to the cement slab. The aluminum-framed windows had to be propped open with small boards. The walls were made of thin, cheap paneling; every word uttered could be heard in the other units.

The tenants propagated copiously in spite of the thin walls.

Each unit had a large space heater. There were no garages or storage sheds. The exterior, which was made of some sort of composite material, was painted baby blue. A lone, misshapen and stunted fir tree stood in the front yard. There were no shade trees.

The apartments were in demand in the community. They were the cheapest rental properties in the area and the poorest of the poor came to rent them. We seldom had to advertise, but spent much time in small claims court trying to collect back rent.

"Don't the tenants in Number 3 owe us rent?" I asked Carsten one morning. He was sitting at the kitchen table in his nightshirt. The morning paper was spread in front of him.

"Two months," he said as he continued reading.

"Two months! Why are they still here? Did you give them notice?" I asked. I knew he hadn't....he never did...I just wanted to rub his nose in it a little.

"Look, they've been having car trouble. They had a big expense for that. Without a car, they couldn't get to work, so they didn't get paid."

I was exasperated. "There's always a reason they can't pay. Why can't they pay us first and then take care of the car?"

"Well, that's just unreasonable. How can they get any money if they can't get to work? You just don't realize what it's like to be poor."

"I'm learning," I said.

"If it bothers you so much, why don't you stop down there on your way to the post office and try to get some money out of them?" Carsten said.

"Why don't you do these things sometimes?" I asked.

"I'm an executive. I don't do things like that." Carsten was only half kidding.

I walked out, slamming the door behind me. The apartments were more trouble than they were worth. I knocked on the door of

Number 3 and could hear people inside but, not surprisingly, no one came to the door.

There was a constant turnover of tenants and their names became blurs. We took to naming them, giving them monikers corresponding to their personality traits. This was helpful for our own identification purposes, but caused problems when we had to write them receipts for their rent, which was always paid in cash. I began just telling them to fill in their own names.

A few tenants were memorable, either because of their sad stories, their brazen nerve or their hopeless situations.

Half-Wit

When I married Carsten, a young girl occupied the front west apartment. She looked too young to be a mother, yet she had two small children, a boy and a girl. The children were about one and three years old. The boy, who was the oldest of the two, was tow-headed and small for his age. He never spoke to us. When we made overtures to him, he became frightened and ran away to hide.

The mother would not be described as beautiful, but had a sweet face and trim figure. She did not work, but paid her rent either from welfare or from the charity of an older sister who was very normal and responsible. Our tenant was reluctant to let anyone into her apartment. We suspected it was filthy. Because of her inability to manage her children or keep her tiny apartment clean, Carsten named her Half-Wit.

Our home addition was not yet complete, so our office was in one of the adjacent apartments. Through the thin walls, I could hear her screaming at the children. She never spoke in a normal tone to them. She soon acquired a new puppy without asking our permission and, in spite of our "no pet" policy, we did not have the heart to make her get rid of it. It was probably the only nice thing she had ever done for the children. She did not know how to care for it any better than she knew how to care for her children. She tied it on a rope and left it in the bright sun with no shade and no water. I told her she had to give the puppy some water.

"He's such a cute puppy," I said. "Every time I pet him he pees. I call him Leaky Puppy."

She glared at me. "Don't never call him that," she said. "That ain't his name." She sneered at me, exposing her gray, unbrushed teeth.

"What should we do?" I asked Carsten after listening to her yell at the children day after day. "Should we notify the child welfare agency? It's not just the screaming. I can see through the windows the place is full of flies and it's January. A new puppy can't help the sanitation problem in there, either."

"The welfare people know about her," Carsten said. "They come out and talk to her every few months. They have to see what is going on. What would you report, anyway? We have never seen her physically abuse the kids. She doesn't neglect them. Hell, she's home with them all day. And, by the way, I think she's pregnant again."

"No way!" I yelled at him. "How could she be? She has no car. She has no job. She never seems to leave the apartment. And how could anyone have sex in one of these tiny apartments with two small kids around?"

"Hey, she doesn't need to have sex. I think her kids are conceived with spunk water and lightning," Carsten said taking another pull on his pipe and returning to his work. He obviously did not want to get involved in the situation.

I felt sick and helpless. I knew the welfare system in the area was notoriously bad. Stories of its shortcomings had been printed in a Chicago newspaper. The social workers probably were aware of the situation and were doing nothing. If she were pregnant, she would probably be even more abusive to the children. The apartment had to be filthy. What would happen to a new baby? I decided Carsten had to be wrong and she was probably just gaining weight.

Unfortunately, a few months later, Half-Wit produced another baby. I again wanted to alert the welfare agency, but Carsten dissuaded me once more. "They really must be aware of the problem now," he said. "They surely saw her in the hospital."

I had to agree and returned to my work, forgetting for the moment the sorry situation next door.

The first of the month came and went and Half-Wit had not paid her rent. Carsten took the receipt book and went to her apartment. I looked up when he came back to the office. His usual ruddy face was white.

"She invited me in while she got the rent money," he said. "I was writing the receipt and I dropped my pen. When I bent to pick it up, I got a whiff of the carpet and I threw up."

"You threw up in her apartment?" I asked.

"No. Luckily I got outside in time."

I didn't know whether to laugh or cry. As time went on, the yelling got worse and I decided I had to call the welfare agency. A new baby should not be in such a filthy place. Even if they did nothing, I would feel like I tried. On the day I was going to make the call, there was no noise coming from the apartment. I wavered. Maybe she was going to improve her parenting skills. I listened again. The walls were so thin I knew I should hear something.

"Listen," I said to Carsten.

"I don't hear anything," he said.

"That's just the point. There is no noise. I'll bet she's gone."

Carsten jumped up and hurried out the door. In a few moments he was back. "You're right," he said. "She's gone."

"Moved out, you mean?" I asked. "Totally gone?"

Carsten nodded. He had trouble speaking. I knew he was regretting we hadn't reported her. "If she moved out of the county, she won't get into the welfare system for a long time and they won't know about her," he said.

I, too, felt a sense of guilt for letting those children down.

The next weekend we began the dreaded job of cleaning the apartment. Along with the flies, we found a few pieces of broken furniture and a mattress. The mattress had a large black spot in the middle which went all the way through to the other side and smelled strongly of urine. The children had been sleeping on the filthy thing. We had to burn it.

Navaho

One of the few tenants who stayed for several years was a large, lumbering woman who spoke and moved slowly and quietly. The fact that she was three-fourths American Indian was apparent in her black eyes and long, straight, black hair. I called her Navaho.

She appeared at our farm seemingly out of nowhere. We had never seen her in the area before and she had no known connections to the community. She was recently divorced and lived with her teen-aged daughter, Paula. Her taciturn manner prevented me from asking her questions, but she sometimes opened up to Carsten.

"My husband was a full-blooded Frenchman," she said proudly, as if he had come with a pedigree. "I had to leave him when he come at me with a knife."

She worked in a small factory in Bradford, paid her rent on time and caused no trouble. She befriended Candy Babcock and found they shared an interest in horses. Soon she asked us if she could have a horse on the property. Carsten once again ignored his "no pet" policy and told her she could. I had to concur with him when she told us Paula had something wrong with her hip and the doctor recommended horseback riding to correct it. She soon acquired a mare, which was kept enclosed by an electric fence in the back yard of the apartment. Navaho took good care of the horse, even though there was no shelter from the weather. She was somehow able to afford to have a veterinarian come out to check on the horse when it was ill. The vet taught her to administer penicillin shots to the horse.

"I don't never get sick," she once told us. "When I feel a cold comin' on, I just give myself a shot of that there penicillin and it goes away."

She approached Carsten one day. "After the combine goes through your field, can I gather the corn it missed for my horse?"

"Of course," Carsten told her.

She looked the quintessential Native American when she walked through the field looking for corn. "My people," I would say as I watched her from my window, "they call it maize."

Eventually, Navaho's mare and Con, the Babcock's stallion, got together and the mare became pregnant. Navaho became almost animated when she talked about the impending birth. She badly wanted a colt and thought she could make some significant money by selling it. Shortly before the birth, the vet came out to check on the progress of the pregnancy.

"When he reached his arm up in her," Navaho said to Carsten, "I wanted to ask if he felt a little pecker in there."

When the foal was born, it did, indeed, have "a little pecker" and Navaho was delighted. She beamed with a rare display of emotion when she told us the good news.

Her joy was short-lived, however. When the colt was only a few weeks old, he was spooked by something and got tangled in the electric fence. He died on the spot. Navaho was heartbroken.

Shortly thereafter, Navaho's mother died. We had never heard her speak of her mother and did not know where she lived. She didn't seem to pay any attention to Navaho or Paula. Navaho, however, inherited a small amount of money, though it did not improve her circumstances enough to enable her to move.

Her grief was soon assuaged by an affair of the heart. She came to our house to pay her rent and seemed eager to tell us something. She did not often spend time discussing her private life with us, but this day was different. She looked down at the ground and tried to stifle a smile. She hemmed and hawed while scraping her foot in the dirt before she could find the words to tell us about her good fortune.

"I been seein' someone," she said. "I don't know if anythin' will come of it, but I hope it will."

"That's nice," Carsten said. "I'm really happy for you."

Navaho looked at him and grinned. It was obvious she thought her life was going to improve soon. "It might mean I'll be movin'," she said.

"Just let us know," I said.

"Who do you suppose she is seeing?" I asked Carsten after she left. "It can't be anyone around here."

"It's probably someone at the factory," Carsten answered.

"I hope he's nice," I said. "She can't have had much good in her life. Her colt died and then her mom. She's hardly a femme fatale, but you never know what attracts two people to each other. Look at me. I fell for you!"

"Fah goo," Carsten said.

When we heard later Navaho's new love was Bad Bill, we knew she was headed for heartbreak again. We could not warn her about him, but watched the situation closely. They were seen together around town and he spent a lot of time at her apartment.

The love affair was brief. When it was over, she settled back into her silent, reticent self and did not talk about what went wrong.

Later, we heard Bad Bill, who knew Navaho had received a small inheritance, asked her to loan him some money. She did as he asked, and shortly thereafter, he dumped her for another woman. Her money was gone and she never got it back.

Hot Pants

A young girl with two small children came to our door one morning, asking if we had a vacant apartment. She explained that her husband was in jail and she had to give up her nice apartment in town.

"His ex-wife accused him of sexually abusing their two kids," she said. "The police came and handcuffed him and led him away, right in front of my kids. Can you believe that? She made it all up just for revenge. He never abused them kids."

Carsten felt sorry for her. "The system just doesn't work for these poor people and they really have no recourse, even when they have been unjustly accused," he told me. We had recently started selling a high school text book about the basics of the law, and with his new found legal expertise, he felt compelled to tell her of her legal options.

She listened to him politely and ignored his advice.

He rented to her and her two small boys without checking any references. She was, after all, a victim. She had a factory job and a small but steady income.

It wasn't long before we noticed lots of new men in the area and they all seemed to be going to the apartments. Our new tenant, it seemed, had a very active social life, even though she was still married to her convict husband. I wondered how she managed to accommodate the men in the apartment with two young children and only one small bedroom.

We named her Hot Pants.

Soon she made friends with a girl in her early twenties, who helped her with the children. Together they acquired a car. It was big, old and gray and had no shine left in the paint. My children called cars like this "ash trays". The hood was very large. Every weekend the two young women would lie on the hood of the car in very skimpy clothing, ostensibly trying to get a suntan, but obviously trying to attract men—-not an easy task in a town of 200 people.

While I was at the store one day Gary, the owner, pulled me aside. "I want to talk to you about your new tenant," he said.

"Do you mean Hot Pants?" I asked.

Gary laughed. "Is that what you call her? Well, I guess that's appropriate, because a guy came in here the other day and said 'I hear there's a girl here in town that's putting out. Could you tell me where she lives?'"

"Let me get this straight," I said between bursts of laughter. "A total stranger came in here and asked if you know where the local girl who 'puts out' lives? That's just unbelievable! Does he think you are running a tourism service?"

"I acted like I didn't know what he was talking about," Gary continued, "but I know he was referring to your tenant."

"I won't tell her," I said. "She would never forgive you for discouraging her visitors."

Some weeks later, I saw a questionable character walking through town with a couple of large garbage bags over his shoulder. They looked like they were full of clothes. I watched him as he went straight to Hot Pants' apartment. He was obviously moving in. Without thinking or even considering asking Carsten about it, I knocked on the door. The man answered.

"If you are planning on moving in," I said, "I suggest you change your mind. This place is not big enough for two adults and two children and I want you out right now."

He looked very startled and started gathering up his things. I watched until he was out of the apartment and off the premises. Carsten later heard the man thought I was Hot Pants' mother.

"You know," I said, "I never even thought to identify myself. I was just too angry. I wondered why he left without an argument."

Hot Pants didn't stay much longer. I don't know where she went. I later met her incarcerated husband's former sister-in-law in Bradford. She told me the child sexual abuse allegations against him were absolutely true.

Lotus Blossom

Carsten couldn't believe his luck when a beautiful Korean woman rented one of the apartments. She was petite and gracious. Delicate strands of gold and jewels hung around her lovely neck. Her earrings were also gold. She was very refined and I wondered how she happened to sink so low as to have to live in one of our apartments.

Her English was not very good and I was reluctant to pry, but over the months I found out a few things about her. She had married an American soldier who had been stationed in Korea and they moved to Bradford where her husband owned a trailer park. They lived in a trailer at the entrance to the park and had three small children. I did not inquire about why she left him, but he now had custody of the children. She worked in a factory.

On the apartment wall hung a picture of her in her wedding dress. It was bright blue silk trimmed in gold braid. Her shiny black hair was twisted into intricate coils. She wore an expensive necklace, lovely pearl drop earrings and several rings. What had she thought on her wedding day? Did she think she would live a life of luxury in America? Had her husband told her about the kind of life they would have? I imagined he had not told her about the sleepy little Midwestern town and the miserable trailer park. My heart ached for her. Occasionally her children came to visit. Otherwise, she seemed to be alone. She had no one to turn to for support. Except, of course, for Carsten. He was at her beck and call. Anything she wanted, he was there for her. Unfortunately for him, she didn't ask for much, but kept to herself.

One morning, while I was getting dressed upstairs, I heard Carsten talking to someone in the kitchen. He seemed very animated and I hurried downstairs to see who was there. It was our lovely Korean tenant. Like most of our tenants, she did not have a phone and had come to use ours. Carsten was busily scrambling some eggs and frying bacon. He was trying to encourage her to have some. The fact that he usually came to breakfast and sat at the kitchen table waiting for me to serve him did not escape me. However, I just smiled. It was an amusing scene. It seems she had to call the factory where she was employed to tell them she could not come to work that day.

"I have trouble," she said. "Have to go to doctor." She hesitated, trying to find the words to explain her malady. "I have something wrong with...with...with my baby grow place."

Carsten stopped scrambling and frying. He quietly turned off the stove and retreated to the office. I was left to help her, which I gladly did. I showed her to the phone and helped her find the numbers for the factory and the doctor.

She moved out of the apartment shortly thereafter. I was sad to see her go. I was afraid she was returning to her husband, whom, I suspect, was abusive. However, she loved her children and I don't think she knew of any other way to get them back.

Ding Dong

The young girl arrived when I was traveling for our business. She came with her mother, who explained this would be her daughter's first time away from home. She had a minimum wage job in Bradford, her first job, and appeared very enthusiastic about living on her own.

"I couldn't check her references," Carsten explained when I asked him about them. "It's her first apartment and her first job. Who could I ask?"

I sighed and merely nodded, knowing Carsten did not like to check references.

"Her mother was very strange looking," Carsten continued.

"What do you mean? Was there something wrong with her?" I asked.

"I don't know. She just seemed lopsided," he explained.

He couldn't explain further, so I let the matter drop. I soon met the girl, a jolly, rotund young lady whose every sentence began with a giggle. She appeared to be so disconnected from reality that I named her Ding Dong. Her mother came by often and I saw why Carsten described her as lopsided. She had had a single mastectomy and did not wear a prosthesis. One large beast was held up by the belt on her cotton dress and there was nothing on the other side.

Ding Dong was at least enthusiastic and wanted to improve her apartment. She told Carsten she would paint the ceiling if he would furnish the paint.

"Isn't that great?" Carsten said, obviously relieved to have someone else do the work.

"Do you think she'll do a good job?" I asked.

"What could she do wrong?" Carsten asked. "It's not a very difficult job." He then bought her two gallons of white paint.

Two days later he decided to see how the painting was proceeding. He knocked on Ding Dong's door and there was no answer. He was very curious about the progress she was making, so he peeked in the window.

"I couldn't believe my eyes," he told me later. "The apartment was empty. She moved out and took the paint. I just gave it to her two days ago."

I was at a loss for words. We never saw her again.

ॐॐ

A few other tenants deserve mentioning. There was the single mother with a toddler and a baby in arms who lived there for a few months. She was sullen, but more attractive than most of our renters and kept her place clean. The toddler was a boy of about two and a half. His head was shaved.

"She's grooming him for the electric chair," Carsten said.

One day Carsten went to collect the rent, as she was often in arrears, and the boy, whose name was Frankie, was on the floor playing with a toy truck. Carsten decided to engage in conversation with him.

"Hi, Frankie," he said. "That's a nice truck you have there."

Frankie, whom we had never heard speak before, looked up at Carsten and scowled. "Shit on you," he said.

Carsten was astounded and related the incident to me.

"Gee," I said," I didn't know he could talk. And here he is talking in sentences already. It must make his mother proud."

The family stayed in the apartment for six months and then moved out of the area. Many years later, the tenant returned and tried to rent another apartment. She did not tell Carsten her name, but she looked familiar to him, and eventually he remembered who she was. Years ago, she had left in the middle of the night owing several months rent, and Carsten called this to her attention. He told her she could not rent from us again, but he asked what had happened to Frankie.

"He's in the Juvenile Detention Center," she said.

We could only think the electric chair might be next.

A young unmarried couple was there for a few months. They were memorable because the girl was extremely young and extremely beautiful. She spoke of her mother and there was sadness in her enormous blue eyes.

"My mother is moving away from here," she said. "She's going with her new boyfriend and they're going to live in Ohio."

"Did she want you to go with her?" I asked.

The girl didn't answer right away and cast her eyes down so I couldn't see the hurt in them. "She told me I'd have to stay here. I have to stay here with Ron. My mother gave up her apartment so I have no other place to live."

"Have you finished high school?" I asked.

"No, I'm only sixteen," she said.

They stayed only a few months. Our neighbors reported seeing them moving things out of the apartment late at night. After hearing this, I stopped by and inquired about their intentions.

"We ain't goin' anywhere," Ron said.

I peered around him and could see the apartment was nearly empty. The beautiful sixteen-year-old sat on the couch inside looking more forlorn than before.

I didn't argue. I didn't want to call the boy a liar. I reminded him he was slightly behind in his rent and then I left. Two days later they were gone.

That beautiful girl had been abandoned by her mother and I could only pray her life would not be ruined.

There seemed to be an underground network of the poor, the unemployable, the unstable in the area. They moved from trailer park to rooming house to our apartments. They knew how to vacate their premises in the middle of the night owing several months' rent. They knew how to avoid small claims court. They knew which landlords were not careful about checking references and work histories. They knew how to disappear. When I talked to other landlords in the area about sharing information, they were not interested. The sharing of information only existed among the tenants. They had us all figured out.

BELLS ARE RINGING

Carsten and I were among the first in our area to sell computer-assisted instruction. Computers were new additions to the schools and often threw the educators into a tailspin. They knew they should have them, but they didn't know why. Some superintendents told us the computers were stored, still in their boxes, in the school basement. Some used them to teach programming. Others used them as instructional tools. That is where we came in. We built up an impressive inventory of instructional materials for the Apple computer. We sold entire courses in English, mathematics, reading and many other subjects.

In addition to software, we sold maps, globes and human body models with removable organs. I sometimes traveled with the plastic human torso model in the front seat of my car.

"Lady! What is that thing?" a teenager in the car next to me once yelled.

I was tempted to copy one of the other salesmen and put a hat on it.

The torso came with interchangeable sex organs. I unwittingly handed a bag of the detached sex organs to a high school girl who was eager to help me carry things into a school for a presentation. When I realized what I had done, I held my breath, hoping she would not look in the bag. I thought she might faint. She did not look.

It had been a long and tiring day when I called on a high school and, without thinking, asked a physiology teacher if he wanted to see my torso.

While traveling throughout Indiana and attending teacher conferences, we met many wonderful and dedicated teachers. Inevitably, there were some who were less wonderful than others.

We occasionally were asked interesting questions such as, "Is this a world globe?" or "Where is Thay-land, anyway?"

At sales meetings the salesmen enjoyed sharing some of their humorous experiences. Among my favorite stories was the one about the teachers' conference in Iowa. This particular salesman was selling text books about different Indian tribes. A teacher approached him and asked, "Do you have any books on the Sigh Ox?" The salesman was baffled and asked her to repeat her request, which she did. Once again, he was mystified until the representative at the next table whispered, "Sioux! She means the Sioux!" The salesman, much relieved, turned to the teacher and said, "We don't have one now, but we will have one ready next month. If you will give me your name and address, I'll send you a sample copy."

She gave him her name and the name of her school. "And what city is that in?" the salesman asked.

"Sioux City," she replied.

Another salesman related a story about one of his favorite customers, a kindergarten teacher. She told him about her experience with a goldfish, which she kept in her classroom.

"The children loved that goldfish," she said, "and they named it Goldie. Then one weekend I came to school to prepare for the next week and Goldie was belly up in the fish bowl. I knew the children would be heartbroken and I didn't know what to do. Realizing most goldfish look alike, I decided I could replace Goldie and no one would be the wiser. I have a bathroom in my classroom, so I flushed Goldie down the toilet and went to the store to buy another fish. On Monday, I put the new fish in the bowl and not a single child knew the difference. I was quite proud of my resourcefulness until a little girl went into the bathroom. After a few minutes she came running out, her panties around her ankles. 'Teacher! Teacher!' she said. 'I just pooped a goldfish!'"

Our travels took us to many schools, both good and bad. Some schools in the worst areas were run by caring and intelligent principals who made the students work hard and encouraged them to succeed. Other schools in the same town were a disgrace. A large city in our territory, once a prosperous manufacturing community, had been abandoned by the blue-collar workers who used to man the factories there and left it to people of color and the very poorest of the poor.

I was asked by one of the companies I represented to pick up some materials it had sent on preview to a high school there. I approached the school cautiously, noting the drug dealers standing right outside the door. I had to get into the school, but the doors were chained and bolted, a clear violation of the fire codes. A sweet young boy who was outside saw my dilemma and asked me if I wanted to get into the school.

"I'll help you, lady," he said and he proceeded to pound on the door, trying to get the attention of the administrator, whom he could see inside through the wire reinforced window in the door.

"Mr. Johnson! Mr. Johnson!" he yelled as he continued pounding.

Mr. Johnson did not react.

"Mr. Johnson! Open up, you mother-fucker!" he yelled. With that, Mr. Johnson turned around and came to the door. "There you are, lady," the young boy said, smiling proudly.

It took no small amount of self-control to thank him for his help without laughing. Inside the school I encountered kids smoking in the stairwells and throwing trash in the halls. The teacher I went to see denied she had ever received any materials for preview. And yet the same school district also had one of the best run high schools I encountered in the state.

The head of the English departments for the school district was housed in the administration building. His skin was a beautiful chocolate brown. His voice was soft and modulated and his motions were slow and fluid, making his entire persona like velvet. He asked me to do a presentation of our English and language arts materials. When I attended the meeting of high school English department heads, he opened the session by turning to me and saying, "We begin every meeting with our special moments." I held my breath. I thought we were going to pray. He continued, "This is when we share special times we have had in the classroom since we last met."

I glanced around the room. There were about six English teachers seated around the table. None of them spoke. When it became obvious no one had experienced a special moment during the last month, Mr. Velvet looked disappointed, but continued with the meeting. The next item on the agenda was the SAT scores. The district had the lowest scores in the state and the state scores were among the lowest in the nation.

"We used to say, 'Thank God for Kentucky,'" one teacher said. "They were always lower than we were. Now we are lower than Kentucky."

I was beginning to feel very uncomfortable. When it was my turn to speak, I tried to use the information I had just heard to my advantage, telling them our software could turn their situation around, but I am not sure I believed it.

Carsten and I traveled around the state for many years and eventually became well enough known to be able to do much of our business from our home. Carsten was adept at making deals over the phone and I did much of the back-up work, including keeping the books, which Carsten would probably never have done had he been on his own. He was always on the lookout for additional ways to make money and he started selling used textbooks to schools that could not afford new books or needed to supplement their supply. Large semis full of books that some schools had discarded began appearing at our house. The drivers miraculously backed the semis up the long gravel driveway, unloaded many cartons of books and then skillfully maneuvered the truck down the winding driveway again. We had no room for the hundreds of books in the house, so Carsten stored them in the still unfinished barn, which now had a roof over one-third of it. It soon was overflowing with books. I could not imagine we would ever sell all of them. What would we ever do with them?

At about the same time, Carsten brought his mother, Florence, from her home in Upstate New York to stay with us. Jeffrey the Great and Martin the Magnificent, disrespectfully and behind her back, called her "The Old One" and we eventually shortened that to "OO". She had come twice before. The first time she came, she was recovering from a broken hip. She had slipped, late one night, on one of the many small throw rugs she had scattered throughout the upstairs of her house and she fell on the hardwood floor. Because her hip was broken and because she had no phone upstairs, she lay on the floor all night. At first light, she dragged herself to the stairs and somehow scooted downstairs to the telephone.

Carsten went out to New York to attend to her after the doctors put a pin in her hip.

He then drove her back to Indiana. Because she lived all of her life in the house she was born in, she was not happy about being uprooted. We had just fixed up the room off of the kitchen to be my separate office, but it became her room.

Her arrival was awkward for her and for me, as this was our first meeting.

Carsten did not tell his mother about me until we had been married for a few months. He even delayed telling Jeffrey the Great and Martin the Magnificent we were married until a month after our wedding. When circumstances arose requiring him to tell them, they said they would never come to the farm again. Carsten was devastated. I knew the threat was an empty one. They would eventually need things like college tuition and gas money. Their mother, Cece, made sure she would never pay for anything. They stayed away a few weeks, and then, out of necessity, relented. Then Carsten had to tell his mother.

Florence was a Catholic, and even though Carsten's now deceased father was not, she let it be known she did not approve of Carsten getting married for the second time. I was a divorcee and not a Catholic. She made it clear she was not going to stay in our house of sin any longer than was necessary.

She made no contributions to our home. She did not try to be sociable or pleasant. She stayed in her room most of the time. We did not expect her to help pay for groceries and she did not offer. I shopped, cooked, cleaned and laundered for her.

My own mother began to have health problems and I sometimes went back to Springfield to help her. While I was gone, OO, who played the invalid when I was home, fixed meals for Carsten and helped with the dishes. One evening, after driving the five hour trip from Springfield, I was surprised to find her in the kitchen, cleaning up after dinner.

"Hello, Florence," I said. "It's good to see you up and about."

She turned and looked at me. "Sarah," she said, "we're out of butter."

OO was once the main breadwinner in her family. She was first a history teacher and then worked for an insurance company. Carsten's dad, who died long before I met Carsten, was described to me as a handsome, charming, brilliant man, who never held a job for long.

"People always asked me what my dad was doing," Carsten said. "When I went out on dates, he would say, 'If they ask you what your father's doing now, just tell them when you left home he was reading the paper.'"

Mr. O'Day never attended college, but was very well read. He also could play the piano beautifully, even though he had never had lessons and could not read music.

"I wanted to play like my dad," Carsten said, "but I never took lessons. My dad told me he began playing in his teens when the talent just came to him. Rather than take piano lessons, I thought I would wait until the moment came when I, too, could just sit down and start playing like he did. It never happened."

OO lived alone but was anxious to go home. She refused, however, to get a telephone installed upstairs in her New York home.

"We will take you home when you get a phone by your bed," Carsten said.

"Why do I need a phone by my bed?" she asked. "Nothing is going to happen to me."

We pointed out the fact that, indeed, something already had happened to her, but to no avail. Carsten finally called the phone company and made arrangements to have us pay for a phone by her bed. He then consented to drive her home. In order to be ready to leave at a moment's notice, she had kept her open suitcase on a table in her room and had never unpacked it. She never put anything in the dresser drawers and when it was time for her to go, she was ready in five minutes. All she had to do was pack her toothbrush and close her suitcase. She had been with us for three months.

After a few months, the telephone company called us and told us it was against their policy to have someone pay for another person's phone and they would have to remove the upstairs phone, which they did. We were back where we started.

We visited her when we could. I was impressed by the neatness of her house. She had things organized well to minimize walking, although the only bathroom in the house was upstairs. Her washing machine was in the kitchen. She had no dryer, but hung her clothes on a drying rack over a heat duct in the dining room. Small boxes were on the coffee table and end tables in the living room. They held sewing supplies, paper clips, pens and rubber bands. A baby grand piano, which she never played, was in the living room. She used it as a place to display cards and pictures people sent her. The cards from Carsten's first wife were always propped up and prominently displayed. The cards and letters I sent her were folded and placed underneath some junk mail.

An ancient gas stove was in the 1940s era kitchen. The burners would not light from the pilot, so she would turn on the gas, shuffle across the room, open a drawer, remove one match, shuffle back across the room to the stove, and make several attempts to strike it. When she finally lit the match, she would hold it up to the burner. It often did not ignite, so she would wave her hand slowly over the flame or gently blow on it. She usually succeeded in blowing out the match before she lit the burner. She then began the entire process all over again while the gas continued to pour out. Each time, she got only one match out of the drawer. After watching her do this several times, I ran into the living room where Carsten was reading the paper.

"Get out of here!" I yelled. "This whole place is going to blow!"

She lit the stove the same way every day and the house never blew up. I wondered if that miracle had anything to do with her ardent Catholicism.

We visited her one Thanksgiving and attempted to cook the holiday dinner in her antiquated kitchen. The oven door refused to stay shut after I put the turkey in. Carsten solved the problem by duct-taping it shut. We replaced the stove shortly after.

☙❧

When Jeffrey the Great was in high school he had a girl friend. She was in his class. Like many of the people in that corner of Indiana, she was of Polish descent.

"I never thought my son would date a girl who had no vowels in her last name," Carsten said.

Jeffrey the Great brought her to the farm to meet his father. He told Carsten they would arrive at noon one Saturday in the spring. I prepared lunch for them. Then Jeffrey called.

"We'll be a little late," he said. "We probably won't be there until around 1:30."

At 1:30 he called again. "I guess it will be closer to 3:00," he said.

"We have lunch here for you," Carsten said. "Will you still want lunch?"

"Yes," Jeffrey the Great said. "But I don't want to eat with Sarah."

Carsten uncharacteristically was offended by this.

"I think I'll put a table and chairs in the yard," he said. "Just let them eat there."

I was tempted to leave, but I was curious to meet a girl who would like Jeffrey the Great. They finally arrived in the middle of the afternoon. The girlfriend was tall, pretty and vacuous. We attempted conversation but were not very successful. She mostly gazed at Jeffrey the Great with her big, brown, cow-like eyes.

Carsten mentioned that we had been playing some tennis. That got Girlfriend's attention.

"Jeffrey has taken up tennis, too," she said. "He's getting really good. He can hit the ball really hard. He just has to work on getting it in the court."

I wanted to explain to her that getting the ball in the court was the whole point of the game, but thought better of it and left the room.

When Jeffrey the Great went to college, he met a very nice girl and asked her to marry him when he graduated. Her name was Colleen. She was bright and friendly—-a welcome relief from the first girlfriend.

The wedding was to be in Albany, New York. Colleen approached me during one of their visits to the farm. She was obviously embarrassed about something.

"I really would like you to come to the wedding," she said. "I don't know what to do."

"Jeffrey doesn't want me there, does he?" I said.

"It's totally unreasonable," she said. "I can't get him to change his mind."

"Look, Colleen," I said. "This is going to be the most important day of your life. I would not dream of doing anything to ruin it. I know this family well enough to know I would not be welcome. Don't worry about it."

Colleen was obviously relieved, but still uncomfortable.

OO was not strong enough to go to the wedding.

"I have a good idea," I told Carsten. "We can drive to Albany together and I can meet Colleen's parents a few days before the wedding. Then I can drive back to your mother's house and stay with her for a few days during the wedding festivities. Your mother could use some help. After the wedding, I could come pick you up and we could drive home together."

"That will never work," Carsten said.

"Why not?"

"Because Cece might see you and have a fit. You have no idea how violent she can be. She would probably create a scene."

"And whose problem would that be?" I asked. "Just let her. It only reflects on her, not on anyone else."

"How could you do that to Jeffrey?" Carsten asked.

I stayed home during the wedding.

OO got along fairly well at her home for a year or two after her first stay at our house, thanks in part to her neighbors, who checked on her daily and took her to the store weekly. Her neighborhood was changing and becoming one of immigrants. Her next door neighbors were East Europeans and spoke with heavy accents. I could never pronounce their names, so I called them Mr. and Mrs. B. Mr. B was loud and demanding and his wife was kind and subservient. Her worn and gnarled hands bore testimony to her hard work. On one of our visits, Mr. B called over the fence to Carsten.

"Hey, Carsten," he said, "you got new wife?"

"Yes," Carsten answered.

"Tell me, "Mr. B continued, "which one better in bed, huh? First wife or second wife?"

One day, Mrs. B phoned us in Indiana to tell us something was the matter with Florence. She had evidently suffered a small stroke. Carsten returned to New York and brought her back to stay with us. Once again, she did not unpack and was ready to go in a hurry after six months.

Her health and strength did not improve and we were appalled at her living conditions when we visited her. We tried, unsuccessfully, to convince her she would be better taken care of at our house.

"Won't you be lonely after we leave?" Carsten asked her as we headed back to Indiana.

"It will be a good lonesome," she said.

She was getting very frail, but she refused to leave her house. We tried ordering Meals on Wheels for her, but she said she couldn't have "those people" in her house. We hired nurses, but she complained about them. She was now ensconced upstairs, because the bathroom was there. We made a makeshift kitchen for her in a spare bedroom. It was probably safer than the one downstairs. She was an accident waiting to happen and Carsten finally went and forcibly brought her back to our house.

This time she was nearly 90 years old and weighed 78 pounds with her winter coat on and her purse in her hand. Her back was bent with osteoporosis, and her spine, which had no meat on it, looked like buttons all the way down to her waist. Once five feet four inches tall, she was now about six inches shorter. She stayed in bed all of the time and wanted us to bring her all of her meals and to sit in her room in the evening while she watched TV. Carsten complied. I didn't.

The day she told us she could no longer walk and would have to use a bedpan was the day Carsten called the visiting nurses. They came and made her walk, something she could do fine with a walker, but she just would rather not do. Then they catheterized her and left, saying they would return in a week. It only took one more day of this before Carsten decided to hire a nurse.

In Bradford there was a nursing home called Murray's Merry Manor. I thought the name was more appropriate for an amusement park. Mr. Murray, the owner, was also a state legislator and was the chairman of the legislative committee that oversees nursing homes. Somehow this little tidbit of information was not disclosed until someone decided to run against him. The people of Bradford felt he had a conflict of interest, and Mr. Murray lost his seat. He still retained ownership of the nursing home.

Carsten hired several Certified Nurse's Assistants from Murray's Merry Manor to take turns helping with his mother. A CNA does menial tasks such as washing the patients' hair, giving them baths and preparing their meals. One of the CNAs was decidedly better than the rest and we asked her to leave Murray's Merry Manor and come to work for us. She readily accepted.

Her name was Kim. She was big and strong and lived in a trailer with her husband and four children. She was pleasant, a hard worker, and extremely poor. I wondered about her husband.

"What does your husband do, Kim?" I asked.

She averted her eyes. I hoped she wasn't going to tell me he was on unemployment.

"He sells this book," she finally answered, "but I want him to do somethin' else."

Since we also sold books, I asked her to be more specific. "What book does he sell, Kim?"

She looked even more embarrassed and again averted her eyes. "How to Make a Million Dollars," she said as she turned and hurried out of the room.

We were pleased with Kim. She worked eight hours a day, five days a week. Her presence relieved me of cooking extra meals for OO and relieved Carsten of having to wait on his mother during the day. Carsten was selling some of the used books now and, since Kim's duties with OO did not require sitting in the room with her all day, she helped him clean and repair the books before he sent them out. She tried to retain her good nature while at our house, but I began to sense there were problems at home. I asked her if she was all right.

"I don't think my baby is right. He just don't do things he should be doin'. I thought he would do gooder by now." Kim had trouble with irregular adverbs. After seeing her baby, who was about twelve months old, I had to agree; he was not doing the things he should be doing at his age. I wondered how God expected someone like Kim to handle all of the difficult situations He handed her.

Kim was very grateful for everything we could give her. Our mattress sagged in the middle so badly I thought Carsten and I were going to come to blows over each others' encroachments. We offered it to Kim and she threw it on top of the old station wagon Carsten had sold her for almost nothing.

"That was the bestest night's sleep we've had in years," she said after the first night of sleeping on it.

Kim stayed with us for about two years, but then disappeared. She left her husband and her family. Her husband never worked full time and I think she was so overburdened she had to get out. She eventually returned to them, but never to us.

We got along by hiring other CNAs, but none were as good as Kim.

OO became more and more demanding and difficult. She had a silver bell, which we put by her bed. She rang it constantly, calling "Took! Took!" her pet name for Carsten. Her false teeth flopped halfway out of her mouth when she called. At my request, my dentist made a special trip out to the farm to evaluate her teeth, but could do nothing.

"Her gums have shrunk so much there is nothing to hold her teeth in," he said. "She must have had false teeth for a very long time."

OO remained in her pajamas all day and got out of bed only to go to the bathroom, but put on her makeup and faux pearl earrings each morning without fail. She spent much time on her appearance and slept with her hand mirror beside her in the bed.

I had some experience dealing with old people. I visited my two aunts often when they became elderly and lost their ability to live on their own. One thing I learned: Everyone needs to feel needed. No one wants to be a burden to their loved ones.

The holidays were approaching and I was preparing for my family to come. I told OO I needed help polishing the silver. This was a lie, but I felt it was something she could do. It would let her feel she was making a contribution. She had to be bored sitting in bed all day. I told her I would put a nice soft chair at the kitchen table. Then I would give her rubber gloves and silver polish. I would put a dish of warm, soapy water on the table for her to wash the silverware in after she polished it.

A few days later, Carsten confronted me.

"What did you ask my mother to do?"

"What do you mean?" I asked.

"She has been fretting for two days and she told me today you expect her to polish all the silver. She doesn't want to do it and has worked herself into a frenzy over it."

I explained my motives and told him to go tell her I decided I didn't need help after all.

A few weeks before Christmas, OO called me into her room. She handed me a twenty dollar bill.

"I want to give Took new pajamas for Christmas. Would you buy them for me?"

I did as she asked and Carsten bought a few things for her to give to the boys. I got a card table and put it beside her bed. I put wrapping paper, scissors and tape on the table.

"I thought you would like to wrap your presents," I said.

She sat up and swung her feet under the table. I left the room.

Fifteen minutes later, she called me back.

"Sarah," she said, "I can't do this."

I wrapped Carsten's pajamas and wrote "From Mother" on the tag. Carsten did not have to wrap my present from OO, because there was none.

We replaced Kim with Billie Jean, also from Murray's Merry Manor. Billie Jean and I sometimes sat at the kitchen table drinking our morning coffee. We could see into OO's room from there. We watched her as she took off an earring and dropped it into the wastebasket by her bed. She then began to ring her bell.

"What can I do for you?" Billie Jean asked.

"I've lost my earring," OO whined.

Billie Jean simply reached into the wastebasket and retrieved it.

"Here it is!" she said, feigning surprise.

Carsten and I were OO's captives in the evenings and on the weekends, as we had no help then and could not leave her alone. One weekend, when Carsten was gone and I was upstairs in the new addition, she began ringing the bell and yelling for someone to come to her room. I ran down the stairs, through the dining room, through the kitchen, around the wood stove, and into her room.

"What do you want?" I asked breathlessly.

"I just wanted to see if anyone was here," she said.

"Have we ever left you alone?" I asked her.

"No, but there's always a first time."

She had very little money but kept close watch over what she had, making sure we didn't take any of it. Of course, we were paying all of the food and nursing care bills. She contended she did not eat enough to make a difference, in spite of the fact that she gained twenty pounds while she was with us. I asked the local beautician, whose son, the rapist, was once again in jail, to come up to the house and fix her hair. When she arrived, OO had a tantrum. She would not let her touch her hair. The beautician, who was used to dealing with cantankerous old women, finally lied and told her there was no charge for her services. OO calmed down and let her cut, shampoo and curl her hair. We surreptitiously paid for it.

OO did not like games. Carsten and I enjoyed Scrabble and Trivial Pursuit, but OO only sneered, "I don't play games." For her entertainment, Carsten got a large wad of one dollar bills and gave them to her. She loved to count them. One night he gave her the bills and we tiptoed out of the house and went shopping. We were gone about an hour and a half. When we returned, she was still counting them. She never knew we had left her alone.

OO had no brothers or sisters. Carsten was an only child, also, so they had very few relatives. April, the daughter of OO's cousin, was just about the only relative she had. April, her husband, and their daughter lived in the same Upstate New York town as OO. We received a phone call from them one evening.

"Carsten," April said, "I hate to bother you with this, but we have had a fire in our home. We are fine, but there is quite a bit of damage to the house. We have to move out for about four months.

Do you think we could move into your mother's house while repairs are being made?"

Carsten told me about it.

"I think that would be wonderful," I said. "Your mother's house needs to have someone in it. April could take care of it and have a free place to live."

Carsten agreed and approached OO with the idea. She couldn't answer right away.

"I'll have to think about it," she said. "I don't think I like the idea."

A few days later, Carsten asked her again. This time she didn't hesitate.

"NO!" she said, and the discussion was over.

OO was starting to get quite deaf and was having trouble hearing the television. TV was about her only source of entertainment. The CNAs had even gotten her interested in the afternoon soap operas. We felt it was imperative to make the necessary adjustments to the television so she could have something to occupy her days and evenings. Carsten set up an elaborate system of speakers in her room, which helped a little. We gave her the remote control and watched in amazement as she did everything possible wrong so it wouldn't work.

"Even if I tried, I couldn't imagine doing that many things wrong," I said. "She points it at the ceiling. Then she points it at herself. She puts her finger over the light. She holds it backwards and sideways. Do you suppose she is trying not to be able to work it so we will have to go in there and change the station for her?" I had trouble talking with my tongue in my cheek.

When she was displeased with us she would pull her catheter out. She told me it just fell out.

"Does it ever fall out when you are in the room?" the visiting nurse asked me.

"No," I said. "It seems to fall out when Carsten is out of town."

The nurse laughed. "After we insert the catheter, we fill a balloon with water. That is inside of her and it has to hurt like crazy to pull the thing out. She is just doing this for attention."

The visiting nurses came twice a week to check on her vital signs and do tests the CNAs were not qualified to do. One of them sat down at our kitchen table one morning after she checked on OO.

"I don't want you to go in her room any more," the nurse said.

"What!" I said. "How can I not go in there? I have to take her dinner in there every night. And on the weekends, we have no help."

The nurse shook her head. "Let your husband do it."

"Why?" I asked.

"I was talking to the other nurse who comes here. We think Florence is the meanest to her caregiver, namely you, of all of our patients. We are afraid you are going to have a breakdown if you continue to put up with her abuse."

I was stunned. "She isn't that bad," I said. "She isn't good, but she could be worse."

"Not much," the nurse said, rising from her chair. "If you can't avoid going in there, just keep it to a minimum."

I never told Carsten. I went into OO's room as little as possible, but there was not much I could do to change the situation.

Late one night, when I was upstairs in bed and Carsten was working in the office, I heard a small commotion and went downstairs to see what was going on. OO was lying on the floor in her room. Her arm was scraped and a large piece of skin as thin as tissue paper was hanging from it. Carsten wrapped her arm in a wet cloth and called an ambulance. After a long time, the ambulance arrived and two obese women in brown polyester pants stretched to their limit came to the door. They had a gurney with them and had a difficult time getting it past the wood stove and into the bedroom. They placed OO on the gurney and then they didn't know how to get it out of the room. After much maneuvering, the deed was finally done and OO was placed in the ambulance. Carsten got in beside her.

"Get dressed and drive my station wagon to the hospital," he told me. "We will have to drive her home after they tend to her and she might have to lie down in the back."

I did as I was told, taking a long time to find his car keys and not bothering to hurry. I knew all I would be able to do at the hospital was sit in the waiting room. It might take hours. I finally left the farm and proceeded into town. I had gone less than a mile when I saw lights up ahead. It looked like an ambulance. I wondered how there could have been two emergencies in this sparsely populated area on the same night. When I caught up to it, I realized this was the ambulance with Carsten and his mother in it. I followed it all the way to the hospital and it never went over fifteen miles and hour.

"What is going on?" I asked Carsten when he got out of the ambulance.

"I asked the same thing," he said, shaking his head in disbelief. "They said there was something wrong with the ambulance and it wouldn't go any faster."

"It's lucky she didn't have anything life-threatening," I said.

We stayed at the hospital until 3 a.m. The surgeon artfully sewed the thin piece of skin back on, a feat I never thought he could accomplish. Carsten remarked that he would be great at tying flies. Fishing was never far from his mind. I sat by OO's bed when the surgeon had finished. Carsten was in the business office doing the necessary paperwork. OO looked at me and smiled.

I smiled back. She's going to thank me for coming to the hospital in the middle of the night, I thought. She's finally going to express her appreciation for all we have done for her.

"This never would have happened if I had been at my house," she said. Then I realized that her smile was actually a sneer.

The next day the visiting nurse came to check on her. "Did you notice she fell on the other side of the room from her bed?" she asked me. "I have always suspected she could walk better than she let on and she probably does some wandering at night."

This was a fact I couldn't refute.

Her condition deteriorated rapidly after her fall. She sat in bed all day, ringing her bell for attention.

"You're going to hear that bell in your head long after she is gone," Amy and Dan told Carsten. He agreed with them.

She started getting bedsores from lying in bed all day and night. I frantically looked for a cure, as I knew they could be very painful. The CNAs applied the lotion I found and, though the sores did not heal, they were kept under control. She began having trouble swallowing. Her head was now down to her chest, her thin little back bent into a bow. It was no wonder food would not go down her bent esophagus. Billie Jean sat by her bed and spoon fed her a drink that was full of vitamins. OO was failing rapidly.

Because OO was part Irish, I gave her a shamrock for St. Patrick's Day. Billie Jean watered it daily. I knew she was drowning it.

"It's really spooky," Billie Jean said to me one day. "The more she fails, the more the shamrock droops. Every day they both die a little bit more. It's creepin' me out."

Soon OO began moaning at night. She moaned so loudly we couldn't sleep. We had no help after 5 p.m. and Carsten especially was getting worn out. He had huge black circles under his eyes.

"Maybe the doctor can give her something to make her more comfortable," I suggested. We called the doctor and he offered to come to the house. He was a personable but lecherous old man with a reputation of sleeping with his nurses. He sat at our kitchen table as we told him OO's symptoms.

"Is there something you can give her to ease her pain?" Carsten asked.

"And we are awake all night with her moaning," I added. "Can you give her something to make her sleep?"

"You just want to help yourself," the doctor said, looking at me. "You aren't interested in helping her."

I was dumbfounded. Yes, we wanted to get some rest, but we also wanted OO to get some sleep. I stared at him in amazement. I looked at Carsten, who, as usual, didn't stand up for me. I was scheduled to talk to a group of teachers in Indianapolis that afternoon, so I simply walked out of the house and drove away. I spent the night in Indianapolis.

That night OO died.

I returned to the farm early the next morning. As I turned into the driveway, a large black van containing two men dressed in dark suits was leaving our house. I knew the van contained OO's body.

Carsten was on the phone when I entered the house. Jeffrey the Great was now in the Air Force and was on a survival training mission. He could not be reached and Carsten made arrangements for the funeral to be delayed until the following week when Jeffrey would be available. The service was to be held in Upstate New York.

When he got off the phone, he filled me in on the plans. "After the funeral, we can finally have some time to ourselves. Let's drive around New York state and just have a leisurely trip home."

"You need that," I said.

"We both do," he answered.

The phone rang. When Carsten went to answer it, I went into OO's room. I picked up the mirror she always had with her and glanced around the room. There were a few things Jeffrey the Great and Martin the Magnificent might like to have. I began putting her belongings into little piles: this goes to the boys; this goes to Goodwill; Billie Jean might like this....

Carsten entered the room. "Martin wants me to meet him for lunch at a restaurant over near his house."

"I thought he might come here," I said. "I'm making a pile of his grandmother's things for him to take."

"He wants me to go there," Carsten said, walking out the door and leaving me alone.

He did not return until late afternoon. He walked into the house without acknowledging me and went straight to the living room where he plopped down in his easy chair.

I followed him. "Okay, what happened?"

He shook his head. "It was unbelievable. I met Martin at the restaurant and he said he was not comfortable talking in a public place. He insisted we go to his mother's house."

"That was probably a good idea," I said. "Cece would be at work and you could have privacy."

"Cece took the day off. She was there. She fixed a big lunch for us." Carsten kept shaking his head as if he couldn't believe it himself. "They both sat me down and said they did not want you to go to the funeral."

I didn't respond. I had never heard of someone being denied the right to go to a funeral.

"I told them you had done a lot for OO." Carsten said. "I told them you should be allowed to come. That I wanted you there."

"Thanks," I said.

Martin the Magnificent called the next day to ask if I was going to the funeral. Then Cece called. Carsten stood his ground.

"I'm really proud of you," I told him after the third day of phone calls. To myself I said, "I wonder how long it will take for him to give in."

Each day brought more calls and each day I watched Carsten lose his resolve a little bit more.

"Are you going to the funeral?" he asked me one day.

"Who wants to know?" I asked. "And why do I have to tell anyone if I am going or not?"

The strain was showing in Carsten's face. The inevitable finally happened after a week. With the help of some Irish whiskey, he said, "I don't want you at the funeral."

Carsten left for the funeral and I stayed home. As soon as he was gone, I called a resale shop.

"I have lots of furniture I want to sell. When can you get here?"

"How about this afternoon?"

"Perfect," I said. "Bring your truck. I want you to take the things today."

When Carsten returned home after the funeral, he entered a half-empty house. I sold only what was mine, but it was a considerable amount. He knew immediately what was happening.

It took some time for me to pack and leave. The day the moving van came, Martin the Magnificent came to be with his father.

"You were mean to my grandmother," he said to me.

I stared at him, unable to speak. OO had told me for years Cece was mean to her. Now it was obvious she had told Cece I was mean to her. How could I explain this to her grandson? He had the impression his grandmother was a sweet little old lady. I thought it should remain that way, so I did not answer.

My son, Dan, went with me. We moved into an apartment in Bradford. It was a temporary move to give me time to decide what to do.

One day, Carsten called me. "Do you remember when your kids told me I would hear OO's bell after she was gone?"

"Yes," I said.

"Well, I kept hearing it," he said. "I heard it every night and I thought I was going crazy. Then I looked in the tree outside my bedroom window and the bell was there. I know Dan hung it there."

Carsten sounded furious. I had a hard time stifling my laughter. That night I asked Dan about it and he confessed.

"I hope OO is looking down at us and is seeing what has happened since her death," I said.

"Mom," Dan said, "maybe she's looking up."

EPILOGUE

Before I got married for the first time, my fiancée and I went to talk to the minister, as was required.

"Why are you getting married?" he asked us.

We both gave the same answer.

"Because I love him," I said.

"Because I love her," he said.

"I had hoped you would say more," the minister said.

I, all of twenty-two years old at the time, could not imagine what more I should have said.

"I had hoped you would say you respected and admired each other. I had hoped you would say you made each other feel good, that you are truly happy when you are together," the minister continued. "Your answer wasn't wrong. You need to love each other. But you need more." He was right.

Carsten and I thought we had more. We thought of things at the same moment. We laughed at the same things. We recognized the same injustices and felt the same pain. Our bodies and minds meshed. I loved to snuggle up to his furry chest and talk until three in the morning. Although individually our appearances were unremarkable, people often commented that we were an attractive couple or we looked happy when we were together.

"I love to see you together," said one educator when we were on a sales call. "I can see the love in your eyes when you look at each other."

Still, it was not enough. Painful incidents that happened before we met seeped into the present. Unresolved disagreements began to taint the relationship.

No one gets married thinking some day they will be divorced. Even though we know the risks and the statistics, we believe it won't happen to us. But happen it does.

Divorce is a very ugly word. It connotes failure, disappointment, sorrow, broken dreams, pain and anger. It is the end of a relationship. When a relationship is ended by death, people gather around the widow or widower and give their condolences and support. Funerals are sometimes called celebrations of life. None of this happens in a divorce. The two parties are left alone in their shame and sadness. Divorce is something all couples try to avoid, and yet there comes a point of no return when you have given all you can give and forgiven all you can forgive. Then divorce, with all of its bad connotations, must be considered.

The realization that our marriage had to end came slowly in bits and pieces...tiny pieces building on top of each other until the weight was too much to bear. I finally realized love was not enough. Those things we each brought with us into the marriage, those things we should have left behind, reared their ugly heads and could no longer be ignored. That was when I realized I had no other alternative but to leave.

I had thought about leaving Carsten before, but always changed my mind. When he told me I could not go to his mother's funeral, he did me a favor, although I could not see it at the time. His egregious act of cowardice and his lack of concern for my feelings made leaving easy. I knew I would never look back.

He sent me a poem:

The mind has a thousand eyes,
The Heart has only one,
Yet the light of a whole life dies,
When love is done.
By F.W. Bourdillon

I knew I did the only thing I could do, but I, too, was sorry love was done. Love is a very curious emotion. When it ends, it is irretrievable. There was no going back to the person with whom I was the most intimate in my entire life.

I stayed in the area for another year, assessing my life and planning my future. Then, one day, when my head was clear, I realized I had to answer the genetic pull of my ancestors and the imprinting on my DNA. I knew I had to return to my roots...to Springfield. I went home again and found a sturdy house no storm could ever harm, unlike the patched-together house I left behind. It was small and brick and it needed much work, a task I now knew I could undertake. The new house was also on a busy street. As I watched the cars go by my kitchen window, I smiled to myself, knowing people were in those cars. I was no longer isolated on a farm near a very small town in Indiana. I was once again in the place where I belonged.

3657731

Made in the USA